SERIES EDITOR: LEE JOHNSON

MEN-AT-ARMS 335

ÉMIGRÉ & FOREIGN TROOPS IN BRITISH SERVICE (2) 1803–15

TEXT BY
RENÉ CHARTRAND

COLOUR PLATES BY
PATRICE COURCELLE

First published in 2000 by Osprey Publishing,
Elms Court, Chapel Way, Botley, Oxford OX2 9LP, UK

ISBN 1 85532 859 3

Editor: Martin Windrow
Design: Alan Hamp
Origination by Grasmere Digital Imaging, Leeds
Printed in China through World Print Ltd.

00 01 02 03 04   10 9 8 7 6 5 4 3 2 1

FOR A CATALOGUE OF ALL TITLES PUBLISHED BY OSPREY MILITARY,
AUTOMOTIVE AND AVIATION PLEASE WRITE TO:

The Marketing Manager, Osprey Direct, PO Box 140,
Wellingborough, Northants NN8 4ZA, United Kingdom
Email: info@OspreyDirect.co.uk

The Marketing Manager, Osprey Direct USA, PO Box 130, Sterling Heights,
MI 48311-0310, USA
Email: info@OspreyDirectUSA.com

Or visit the Osprey website at: **http://www.osprey-publishing.co.uk**

Dedication

To Christophe

Author's note

The British forces mobilised against Revolutionary and Napoleonic
France throughout nearly twenty years of what was virtually a world
war from 1793 to 1815 included a number of French Royalist
'émigré' units, as well as many foreign corps of various other
nationalities. As will be seen in this and the previous volume (MAA
328, covering the period 1793-1802), many of these units served
not only in Europe – particularly southern Europe – but also in the
West Indies, Africa and Asia. This second volume deals with the
period from the resumption of hostilities in 1803 to the final exile of
Napoleon in 1815. Many formations from this period are little
known, and are presented here for the first time.

With regards to the hues of the uniform colours described, blue
and green were meant to be very dark shades. Red ranged from the
brick red of the common soldiers to a fine scarlet for officers. White,
especially for waistcoats and breeches, could assume a creamy
colour.

Acknowledgements

We gratefully acknowledge the assistance given by Giancarlo Boeri,
William Y.Carman, Randolph Jones, Jacques Ostiguy, the Anne S.K.
Brown Military Collection at Providence, RI (USA) and the Public
Records Office at Kew (UK).

Artist's note

Readers may care to note that the original paintings from which the
colour plates in this book were prepared are available for private
sale. All reproduction copyright whatsoever is retained by the
Publishers. All enquiries should be addressed to:
Patrice Courcelle, 38 avenue de Vallons, 1410 Waterloo, Belgium
The Publishers regret that they can enter into no correspondence
upon this matter.

OPPOSITE **There could hardly be a more suitable example to
dramatise the wide range of troops paid by the British
government than this officer of the 1st Regiment, Greek
Light Infantry, in 1812. He wears a red skull cap with a
black tassel under a white and yellow headband tied on the
right. His short red oriental jacket has red cuffs and is decorated with yellow or gold lace and many small silver
buttons, worn open over a red waistcoat with yellow/gold
lace. He has a crimson sash (perhaps the British officers'
type?) over his right shoulder, and a waist sash coloured
here a more scarlet shade. The white *fustanella* kilt is worn
over white breeches - note the gold or yellow knee bands
and disks. Red stockings trimmed with yellow or gold are
worn with short black boots with yellow trim or top fringes;
the gilded sabre is carried in a crimson scabbard with gilt
fittings. See also Plate D. (Print after Goddard)**

ÉMIGRÉ & FOREIGN TROOPS IN BRITISH SERVICE (2) 1803–15

BRITAIN'S FOREIGN ARMY

FROM 1803 TO 1815 foreign corps represented a sizeable proportion of the British forces. It is difficult to arrive at reliable statistics; compilers of the time did not include the 60th, the 97th, nor the King's German Legion artillery as foreign troops, but did include Canadian Fencible units – which had very few foreigners in the ranks. While not precise, however, the numbers below probably evened out in a general way. In January 1804 the so-called foreign units amounted to some 17,000 men or about 11% of the army. In 1808 this had grown to some 35,000 men or 18% of the army. By September 1813 it reached a peak of nearly 54,000 foreigners, representing more than one man in five in the British army. Thereafter their numbers decreased rapidly until the end of the Napoleonic Wars. In terms of losses, between June 1803 and January 1814 the foreign corps suffered 16,000 deaths in battle or by sickness; 11,600 lost by desertion; and another 10,000 men discharged, many of them invalided out.

There were striking differences in the type of corps and the nationalities of foreign soldiers in the British forces during the period 1803-1815. The French émigré units described in Men-at-Arms 328 all but disappeared; only the Chasseurs Britanniques remained, although now mostly recruited from deserters from the French army. Many French émigré officers were now found scattered in various foreign regiments. Another feature was the near absence of cavalry units, so numerous in the pre-1802 period.

Most noticeably, between 1803 and 1814 new sorts of 'émigré' refugees came to the British forces from the Mediterranean. The Calabrian, Sicilian, Italian, Maltese and Greek levies were foreign units with distinct national characters. Their officers and men were often patriots hoping to oust Napoleon's troops from their native lands with British help. The interior management of units was usually carried on in the corps' dominant language, but key commands and drill orders were given in English in order to avoid confusion as much as possible when foreign units were brigaded with British regiments on campaign.

Readers may be surprised to encounter in these pages many so-called 'colonial' units, but they were equally foreign. Captured territories were by no means certain to remain British. Indeed, one of the reasons for the declaration of war in 1803 was Britain's reluctance to hand back Ceylon (now Sri Lanka) to Holland. The Cape of Good Hope was taken in 1806, La Réunion in 1809, Mauritius in 1810, Java in 1811 – all places where the British immediately raised units.

3

The most spectacular attempt by fanatical Royalists to assassinate First Consul Napoleon Bonaparte was George Cadoudal's 'infernal machine', which barely missed the future emperor in December 1800. These sorts of incidents were generally believed by Napoleon to have been sponsored with British money. (Print after JOB)

As can be seen by the many units listed below, the contribution of foreign units would seem to be more important than previously believed. The King's German Legion and the Brunswick-Oels Corps have justly become well known due to their distinguished service with Wellington's army in the Peninsular and Waterloo campaigns. However, it will be seen that the contribution of Italian troops in the Mediterranean has certainly been somewhat overlooked by historians. There were five Italian regiments, and several other units – such as the Royal Corsican Rangers – with high proportions of Italian officers and enlisted men. Similarly, the many units in Malta and Ceylon stood guard in key stations, thus allowing more British line regiments to be deployed elsewhere. Recruiting in the Balkans produced rather unequal results, as will be seen from the entry on Froberg's Regiment, but two Greek regiments were later raised, with some Croat units late in the war.

British line infantry units which had a high proportion of foreigners such as the 60th, the 97th and the Royal African Corps, are also listed. We have favoured here the lesser known units while referring readers to other studies on corps such as the King's German Legion, wishing to use our limited space to give as much previously unpublished data as possible.

REGIMENTS AND CORPS 1803-1815

The units existing between 1803 and 1815 are listed below in alphabetical order, each with a short account of its history and notes on its uniforms, where known. In some cases further information is given in the previous volume of this study (MAA 328, on the corps active in 1793–1802), or will be found in other existing Men-at-Arms titles cited:

60th Regiment of Foot The 60th was considered as something of a 'foreign legion' in the British infantry. All of its battalions had alway contained strong foreign elements, particularly Germans and Swiss. The first four battalions consisted of line infantry, were armed with muskets, wore red coatees and had white accoutrements. Each had a green-clad rifle company.

The *1st Battalion* was in Jamaica from 1800 to 1810, thence to England and on to the Cape of Good Hope from 1811 to 1819. It was noted as being made up entirely of foreigners except for nine men when inspected at the Cape in July 1815. The *2nd Bn* was in Barbados, Tobago and St Vincent from 1800 to 1807; in Jersey and Spain in 1808, leaving Coruña for Guernsey and on to Barbados in 1809, Guadeloupe and Martinique from 1810 to 1812, and Barbados from 1813 to 1817. The *3rd Bn* was in Tobago, Barbados and Grenada from 1795 to 1809, and in Antigua, Martinique and Guadeloupe from 1810 to 1815. The *4th Bn* was in the West Indies from 1788 and in Jamaica from 1803 to 1805, when it was sent to Lymington, England. Shipped to the Cape of Good Hope from 1806 to 1808, it returned to Barbados, Martinique and Guadeloupe from 1808 to 1810; to Lymington again in 1811, then out to Dominica from 1812 to 1816.

The last four battalions were light infantry, armed with rifles for the 5th and muskets for the 6th, 7th and 8th Bns, each of the last three battalions also having two rifle companies.

The *5th Bn* went from Surinam to Halifax, Nova Scotia, from 1803 to 1805. When reviewed in Halifax during September 1804 it was reported with a strength of 585 foreigners and one lonely Irishman. It was shipped to Portsmouth and thence to Cork, Ireland, from 1805 to 1808; to Portugal and Spain from 1808 to 1814, where it served with distinction with Wellington's army; into France, and back to Cork in 1814.

The *6th Bn*, raised in 1799 on the Isle of Wight, was sent to Jamaica in 1800, where it remained until 1817 and was disbanded at Portsmouth the following year. The *7th Bn* was raised in Guernsey in September 1813 from German prisoners of war; sent to Halifax and on to the present American state of Maine in 1814; back to Halifax in 1815, until disbanded in 1817. The *8th Bn* was formed at Lisbon in November 1813 from the Foreign Recruits Battalion (qv); sent to Gibraltar in 1814, it was disbanded in 1816.

Uniform: See illustrations. 7th Bn: same as 5th Bn. The bayonet belts were to be worn around the waist, as the 5th Bn, instead of over the shoulder. 8th Bn: a 'green rifle uniform' probably the same as the 5th Battalion.

Bourbon Regiment Shortly after the capture on 8.7.1810 of the French island of La Réunion, which had been named Île de Bourbon until the French Revolution, the British authorities raised a local infantry regiment of two battalions under LtCol Henry Keating, 56th Foot. It was intended to recruit the 1st Bn from the white inhabitants

There was great outrage in England and other European courts at the kidnapping of the Duke of Enghein by a party of French dragoons in Germany, but their protests were to no avail. The duke was suspected of involvement in a Royalist conspiracy; Napoleon had him brought to Vincennes castle near Paris, where after a quick 'trial' he was executed by firing squad at 4a.m. on 21 March 1804. For many, this act of judicial murder was the incident which opened their eyes to the true nature of Napoleon's regime. (Print after JOB)

Following the execution of the Duke of Enghein in the moat of Vincennes castle, it was Napoleon who had this sombre monument put up on the spot where he died. It consisted of a pillar with the top cut off – a clear warning signal to those who plotted against his regime.

and the 2nd amongst the free blacks. With the fall of Mauritius (called Île de France by the French) to the British on 3.12.1810 recruiting was extended to that island, but it was found that few whites and free blacks wished to join. The original plan was altered to raise both battalions with purchased slaves, most of whom came from Madagascar; thus the Bourbon Regt was recruited from East African blacks. The officers were mostly British with four others bearing French names (but one of these, Jacques Dupéron Baby, was actually a French-Canadian). In April 1812 the 1st Bn had only three officers and 64 men while the 2nd had 24 officers and 598 men. The regiment was taken on the British establishment from 25.1.1812 as a single battalion unit with an official strength of 34 officers and 642 other ranks in eight companies. It was erroneously named the 'Bourbon Rifle Regiment', but only its light company was armed with rifles. It was not really a light infantry unit either, as it was trained in line infantry manoeuvres.

From 1810 the regiment was stationed on La Réunion. In February 1811 a detachment participated in obtaining the surrender of the French post at Tamatave on Madagascar. In November a slave insurrection occurred at St Leu on La Réunion, but was quickly put down by the planters. Detachments of this black regiment were later used to escort the ringleaders to their execution – a message to the slave populace. In the middle of 1812 the corps moved to Mauritius. In May 1815 the regiment embarked for Barbados in the West Indies.

On 4.4.1816 orders were given for its disbandment, the officers to be sent home and the men to be incorporated into the 1st West India Regiment. However, on 14 April a slave revolt broke out in the parish of St Philips and troops were immediately sent off to the area; two companies of the Bourbon Regt, including the Light Company, formed part of the columns, acting as forward skirmishers. On the evening of the

OPPOSITE **The battle of Maida on 4 July 1806, won by Sir John Stuart over a large French force under Gen Reynier, put an end to French efforts to occupy Sicily. It was the first victory by British arms over a French army on the Continent, and thus brought great encouragement to Napoleon's foes. (Print after De Loutherbourg)**

BELOW **British troops charge the French at Maida. Among the British force were a large contingent of foreign troops including the Sicilian Regiment, the Royal Corsican Rangers, Watteville's Swiss and three companies of the Chasseurs Britanniques. (Period print)**

15th they came in contact with some 400 insurgents, who were under the impression that black troops would not fight them; nevertheless the insurgents fired, killing a private and wounding a sergeant. The Bourbon Regt fired a volley and charged the rebels, killing about 40, capturing 70 and scattering the rest, which ended the rebellion. The Bourbon Regt was then disbanded on 24.4.1816. *Uniform*: See Plate F.

Brunswick-Oels Corps See MAA 167 *Brunswick Troops 1809-15*.

Calabrian Free Corps Raised from early 1809 with Italian refugees from Calabria, some 400 having gathered in Sicily by February in 'centuries' under their own chiefs. At the end of June the corps participated in the raid on Naples, a detachment of about 40 men distinguishing itself in a charge on landing. It participated in the capture of Ischia and Scilla. Back in Sicily, regulations were drafted for the unit's better organisation and discipline. The centuries were re-organised into company-size 'free corps' of three officers, eight sergeants and 120 privates each, and there was a staff of British officers. The company officers, NCOs and privates were to be Calabrian or of the Kingdom of Naples.

On 22.3.1810 some 316 men – after initially wavering – participated with distinction in the attack on the Ionian island of Santa Maura. From December 1812 two divisions of the corps were in eastern Spain, and fought well at Castalla and Biar (April 1813). Consequently, Lord William Bentinck considered the Calabrians to be perhaps the best light infantry in the Mediterranean, in spite of having some 'low-bred, bad Calabrese officers'. At that time the strength reached 1,450 men; six

Map of Calabria and northern Sicily. This area became one of Britain's toeholds in a Europe dominated by Napoleon. The Kingdom of Naples or of the Two Sicilies had been taken over by Napoleon in 1806; he first installed his brother Joseph as king, then Marshal Murat from 1808 when he transferred Joseph to the throne of Spain. Naval superiority allowed the British to secure Sicily and they often operated on the Calabrian mainland. Sicily remained an important base of operations for Anglo-Italian troops until the end of the Napoleonic Wars.

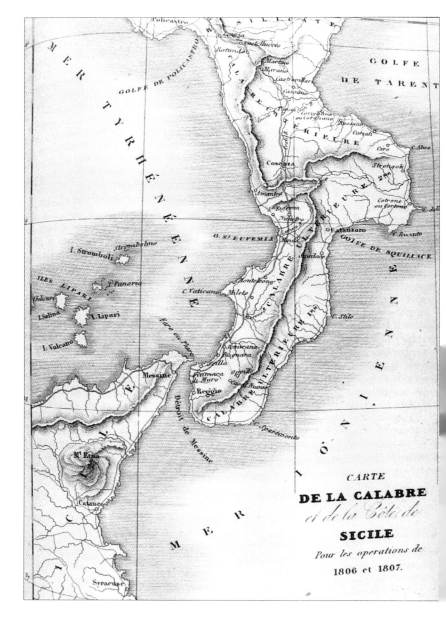

CARTE
DE LA CALABRE
et de la Côte de
SICILE
Pour les operations de
1806 et 1807.

companies were in Spain, six in the Ionian Islands, and three in Sicily. Two companies from the Ionian Islands took part in the siege and capture of Trieste in October 1813, distinguishing themselves by their bravery. The companies in Spain, 579 strong, saw further action at Ordal (12-13 September). In April 1814 these six companies embarked at Tarragona, landed 618 strong at Leghorn, and took part on the British attack on Spezzia on 25-26 March; the garrison surrendered on the 30th. On 14 April the Calabrian Free Corps was part of the force investing Genoa. On the 16th, with the 1st Greek Light Infantry (qv), the regiment carried the high ground above forts Richelieu and Tecla which led to Genoa's surrender later that day. With the war ending, the corps was disbanded from the middle of 1814.

Uniform: The corps' regulations of 1809 specified that each soldier was to be issued every year a jacket of blue cloth with lining throughout, a blue waistcoat, a pair of pantaloons of good strong cloth, a pair of black three-quarter gaiters, a felt shako and a blue cloth forage cap lined with leather. The clothing was to be in the style of light infantry and rifle corps. See page 44 and Plate D.

On 19.10.1811 suits of clothing and greatcoats for 1,240 rank and file and 100 sergeants were shipped from England to Sicily. The suits consisted of jackets, pantaloons, half-gaiters, shakos with plates and plumes constituting the 1812 issue. There were also 20 shoulder knots of gold for staff sergeants and 10 yards of gold lace for chevrons. A Goddard print published in 1812 showed a private in what has sometimes been interpreted as a blue-green jacket, but which must have been meant to be blue, with a yellow collar and cuffs, three rows of pewter buttons on the breast merging into one row at the bottom and edged with white piping, white pantaloons, black half-gaiters, black cylindrical shako with brass bugle horn plate and green plume, musket with black accoutrements and brass belt plate. The uniform style may have changed in about 1813. In a manuscript notation to his printed schematic uniform charts of 1814 Charles Hamilton Smith added the 'Calabrese Corps' in a blue coatee with yellow collar and cuffs, white buttons in two rows on the chest connected by white tape, and blue pantaloons. An inspection of May 1813 mentions that the men wore old pantaloons of 'different colours, viz blue, green &c' as new ones had not been sent (PRO, WO 27/118).

For the buglers, the 1811 shipment included 60 jackets consisting of 83 yards of green cloth (1.38 yards per jacket), 66 yards of grey cloth (1.1 yards per jacket, probably for the lining), 276 dozens of buttons (55 buttons per jacket), 6 gross of lace (presumably 144 yards of lace to a gross, giving 14.4 yards of lace per jacket), and 1 gross (2.4 yards per jacket) of green braid (PRO, WO 1/885).

According to Goddard's 1812 print, the officers wore scarlet jackets with yellow collar, cuffs and turnbacks, three rows of gold buttons on the chest connected by flat gold lace, crimson sash, white pantaloons, black boots, black cylindrical shako with small gilt plate and green feather. The scarlet jacket is very unusual and was probably eventually changed to the same colour as the men's.

Cape Regiment Raised from late January 1806 at the Cape of Good Hope in South Africa following its capture from the Dutch. The regiment had ten infantry companies of 58 officers and men each; formed with Hottentots, many of whom had been in Dutch service, it was now led by British officers. The Hottentots were considered 'perfect as Light Infantry', being 'used to the bush', noted LtCol Graham, adding that they were a good and cheerful set of men who were 'fond of music' (PRO, WO 1/635). A troop of light cavalry was later raised and attached to the regiment. The bulk of the regiment was disbanded on 24.9.1817 except for a small force of infantry and the cavalry being retained to patrol Cape Colony's eastern frontier. It was eventually re-organised as the Cape Mounted Rifles in 1827.

Uniform: See Plate B. Its regular uniform, first received from 1808, was green jacket with black collar and cuffs, three rows of pewter buttons on

ABOVE **Brass plate for the 1800 stovepipe shako. This type of plate was worn by most foreign units from 1803, few if any having gone to the expense of having a special regimental pattern made. (Private collection)**

BELOW **Officer's gilt plate for the 1812 shako, the basic pattern with the double GR cipher. Some foreign regiments added a scroll bearing the name of the unit below the cipher. (Mr & Mrs Don Troiani Collection)**

the breast, green pantaloons, shako with white metal bugle horn and green plume – generally the same dress as the 95th Rifles. The black facing cloth was not included in the 1809 issue but was sent later on. A notation of c.1816 by Pearse mentions for the 'Cape Natives... infantry' $2^{1}/_{2}$ yards of broad lace, 7 yards of cord and 12 hooks and eyes, 'Great Coats Regulation Gray'. The 'musick suit' for the 20 buglers had 15 yards of 'midlin royal braid' and 20 yards of narrow braid. Accoutrements were black, and said to be very good and the muskets in good repair in 1809 (PRO, CO 48/3 and 5; WO 27/ 92 and 97). The officers' uniform was the same as the 95th Rifles. The troop of light cavalry had a green dolman with black collar and pointed cuffs, three rows of pewter buttons on the chest, black cords, green pantaloons with black stripe, green sash at waist with two black stripes, black shako with white band at top, green plume and indistinct round white-black-white cockade, plain black sabretache, and green housings edged with a wide black lace. In 1816 Pearse further mentions for the 'Cape Natives' a 'dress jacket' apparently for cavalry with $2^{1}/_{2}$ yards of broad lace, 9 yards of cord, 12 hooks and eyes and 4 black buttons. There were also 'Cloaks Regulation'[1].

Ceylon Infantry Regiments (See also MAA 328). Regiments raised in Ceylon (now Sri Lanka) were on the British regular army establishment, not the local colonial establishment. By the end of 1804 they stood at 5,401 men – which was more than the King's German Legion, or all eight West India regiments at the same date. However, this was reduced after the end of the war with Kandy in 1805. There were eventually four regiments, numbered from 1805, and each was quite distinct in its character, largely due to the varied origins of the recruits.

The *1st Ceylon Regt* was commanded by Josiah Champagné, a French émigré officer who had served in the 60th Foot. It had 20 British officers, 22 native officers, two warrant officers and 1,087 native enlisted men, largely Malays, in ten companies including one of rifles. It was thus named 'HM Malay Regiment'. The regiment was intensely engaged in the bloody 1803-05 war against the kingdom of Kandy in the centre of the island, and suffered heavy casualties. From June 1814 it became a light infantry corps and adopted light infantry drill. On 10.1.1815 war broke out again against Kandy; this time the British moved in with eight mixed columns of British and Ceylon troops and finally brought the whole island under their rule. The rifle company did especially well, as it captured the King

OPPOSITE **Capt John Robertson, Rifle Company, 2nd Battalion, 60th (Royal American) Regiment of Foot, c.1800-1806. This battalion spent most of the period in the West Indies, with a brief interlude in Spain in 1808. The rifle companies of the 60th's line battalions had green uniforms. The officers, as shown by this portrait, wore the standard coatee rather than a dolman. Green coatee with scarlet collar, cuffs and lapels; silver buttons; green wings and shoulder straps edged with scarlet lace having silver beading at the centre, silver fringes to the wing, and a gilt bugle on a scarlet patch on the shoulder strap; black shoulder belt with silver belt plate with gilt bugle horn. (Chateau de Ramezay Museum, Montreal)**

BELOW **Britain's foreign troops were often involved in naval landing operations in collaboration with the Royal Navy, especially in the Mediterranean. Although some special craft were occasionally used, landings were usually made from ships' longboats manned by sailors, probably much as in this evocative later print by R.Caton Woodville.**

of Kandy on 19 February. The unit became the Ceylon Rifle Regt in 1827.

The *2nd Ceylon Regt* was raised in 1802 by Col William Ramsay and was 1,200 strong in ten companies including one of rifles. Initially it recruited among the Sinhalese, but later accepted numbers of sepoys from Madras; it was known as the 'Ceylon Native Infantry'. An inspection at Colombo on 21.6.1814 found the corps 'very favorable' and noted that 'colours given out to [the] Regt in 1813 [were] totally worn out' already (PRO, WO 27/132). It participated in the 1815 and 1818 campaigns against Kandy, and was subsequently disbanded in 1821.

The Caffre Corps was raised in 1803 from blacks from east Africa. It was disbanded in 1805 and its men transferred to the new 3rd Ceylon Regiment.

The *3rd Ceylon Regt* was raised in early 1805 from recruits obtained in Molucca and Penang and was organised as a regiment under the command of Col Charles Baillie. The black soldiers of the Caffre Corps were incorporated into the 3rd and, by 1814, it was reported to be composed entirely of blacks. This ten-company regiment took part in the 1815 campaign against Kandy, and was disbanded in 1817.

The *4th Ceylon Regt* was raised in 1810 and put on the establishment from January 1811 under the command of Col John Wilson. It had 400 men, nearly all blacks except for a Malay company. The Africans were taught English and many also became Roman Catholics. The regiment took part in the 1815 campaign against Kandy and was disbanded later that year, its men being incorporated into the 3rd Regiment.

Sergeant, Grenadier Company, 2nd Bn, 60th Regiment of Foot, c.1803-1811. (Print after a sketch by P.W.Reynolds from a German engraving)

Uniform: The uniforms of the Ceylon regiments generally resembled those of the British infantry, but their red coatees had unlined sleeves. The enlisted men had white pantaloons and white undress jackets. They were bare-footed and had no issues of shoes, although sandals were worn. The rifle companies were clothed in green. The headdress of the enlisted men varied early on, the 1st, 3rd and 4th having the British infantry shako and the 2nd turbans. The officers' lace for the 3rd and 4th Regts was given in Hamilton Smith's charts as silver (or left blank), but Herbert's lace books show actual orders of gold lace and buttons for officers' uniforms of all four regiments. Accoutrements were white except for the flank companies which had black. The regimental details were as follows:

1st: See Plate F.

2nd: Red coatee, green collar and cuffs, white turnbacks, white lace square-ended and single-spaced, pewter buttons. Light green material was used in 1803 for the facings but became dark green later on. The sepoys being Buddhists, they refused to wear shakos and had blue turbans with yellow ornaments. Gold buttons for officers; turnback ornaments, gold double crow's-foot on dark green. Did not receive clothing between 1810 and 1814. Worn out white accoutrements replaced by black ones in 1812 (PRO, WO 27/118, 123 and 128). The regimental facings were changed to bright yellow in 1818. For the Rifle Company see Plate F.

The Caffre Corps of 1803-1805 was issued with blue cloth, smaller quantities of red cloth and also red with yellow cloth (PRO, CO 54/16).

3rd: Red coatee, yellow collar and cuffs, white turnbacks, white lace square-ended and single-spaced, pewter buttons.

Gold buttons for officers. Between 1808 and 1815 uniforms were received only for 1811. Reported in white jackets, white and blue pantaloons, black accoutrements in 1814 (PRO, WO 27/123).

4th: Red coatee, white collar and cuffs, white turnbacks, white lace with a red line square-ended and single-spaced, pewter buttons. No issues between 1811 and 1814. Gold buttons for officers; turnback ornaments, gold double crows-foot on scarlet.

Ceylon Light Dragoons Organised from October 1803, having a cadre of British officers, NCOs and a dozen native troopers with another dozen from the Madras Governor General's Body Guard. By 1805 it was up to 40 British and 87 natives, taking part in raids against Kandy in 1804-05 and later patrolling the area. The corps was much reduced in numbers, having only 3 officers and 21 men in 1818; but it was not disbanded until October 1832. *Uniform*: This appears to have been a blue jacket or dolman with yellow cuffs and collar (PRO, CO 54/16).

Ceylon Lascars From late 1801, three companies of 'gun lascars' – natives who were essential for the transport and service of artillery in Asian countries – were to be raised in Ceylon. The local Sinhalese were not too enthusiastic; recruiting was slow and by 1804

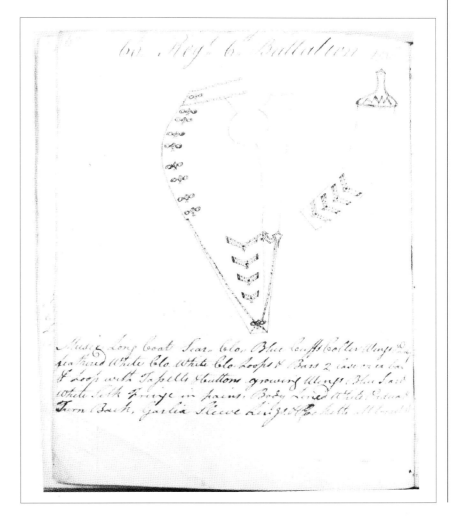

Officer's silver plated and engraved shoulder belt plate, 60th Regiment of Foot, c.1812-1815.

about 400 had been raised in Bengal and sent out to Ceylon. That year 'jackets and turbans for the Gun lascars attached to the Royal Artillery' were made (PRO, CO 55/35). Three companies of Pioneer Lascars raised at about the same time were issued emerald green cloth and equipped with picks, axes and other tools.

Chasseurs Britanniques (See also MAA 328). The regiment was brought to England in 1803 to incorporate other émigrés on the Isle of Wight, and then sent on to Malta. In 1804 its seven-company establishment was raised to the usual ten including two flank companies. From November 1805 the corps was in Naples, until transferred to Sicily in January 1806. In June and July it campaigned in Calabria but was not at the battle of Maida. However, three companies were part of the British force that captured Regio on 9 July; incorporating over 300 French prisoners, the unit was back in Sicily by September. It sailed in March 1807 with the British expedition to Egypt, which proved disastrous: the Chasseurs suffered some 300 casualties covering the retreat on 31 March. The unit remained in Alexandria until September, incorporating some of the officers and men from Froberg's corps(qv). It then went to Sicily and absorbed other groups of foreigners. The corps participated in the raid on the island of Ischia and Scilla on 24 and 30 June 1809.

In November 1810 the unit had some 1,740 men in 12 companies when sent to Cadiz, Spain, where two companies were left until 1813 serving with the Foreign Recruits Battalion (qv). The corps went on to Lisbon in January 1811 and joined Wellington's army in March. It saw much action in the Peninsula, starting at Fuentes d'Onoro (4-5.5. 1811) where Wellington noted its bravery. Other actions were the first attempt on Badajos (7-10 June), Ciudad Rodrigo (19 January 1812), Larena (19 March), siege of Salamanca (21-28 June), Retiro (16 August), Olmos (20 October), Vittoria (21 June 1813), Pyrenees (30 July), Bidassoa (31 August), Nivelle (10 November), Nive (9 December) and Orthez

Rifleman, 5th (Rifle) Bn, 60th Regiment of Foot, c.1812-1815. Two soldiers who deserted at Halifax in June 1805 wore 'a black felt cap, with a black hackle feather, a green regimental jacket, with red cuffs and collar, light blue pantaloons, and regimental gaiters' (*Nova Scotia Royal Gazette*, 6 June 1805). The uniform was generally a green jacket with red collar and pointed cuffs, one row (augmented from c.1808 to three rows) of pewter buttons on the breast, and a white waistcoat. Light blue pantaloons were changed to dark blue from April 1806, and authorised to be green from July 1812, although blue actually appears to have been worn for some time thereafter. Black half-gaiters, and a shako with a white metal bugle badge and green plume and cords completed the uniform. In c.1810 the clothier Pearse made privates' jackets with 44 buttons, buglers' jackets also had 44 buttons, with '30 yds of mixt cord' and '5/8 of worsted'. (Print after P.W.Reynolds)

officer, 5th Bn, 60th of Foot, 1812. Officers had a green dolman with scarlet collar and pointed cuffs, three rows of silver ball buttons and black cords; a crimson light infantry sash with crimson cord; blue overalls and ornamented pantaloons, and hussar boots. The Tarleton helmet was the official headgear for officers until replaced from 1812 by a black felt shako with a silver bugle horn badge and green plume. The green pelisse with silver ball buttons, black cords and fur edging was also adopted at that time. However, the shako and the pelisse may have been in use by some officers before 1812. The officers' greatcoat was green with scarlet collar and pointed cuffs and three rows of silver ball buttons on the chest. The 5/60th served in Nova Scotia and Ireland before, famously, fighting in Wellington's Peninsula army, usually in companies detached to thicken up the skirmishing line of various formations. Print after P.W.Reynolds)

(27 February 1814) – the last major battle. Napoleon's popularity was now eroding fast, and when the Chasseurs Britanniques arrived at Bordeaux escorting the Duke of Angoulème on 12 March 1814 the city had turned Royalist.

By then there were few émigrés left in the regiment except for officers, the rank and file being filled with 'professional deserters' from all over Europe. Desertion had become rampant in the corps, some 224 men taking leave in 1813; it was not allowed to post pickets for fear they would desert. However, in battle they proved steady, often suffering heavy casualties. Following Napoleon's abdication the British troops started to evacuate France and the Chasseurs Britanniques left Bordeaux in July for England. A detachment served as marines on board HMS *Ramillies* off the American coast during the summer. The regiment was disbanded at Lymington on 5.10.1814. *Uniform*: See Plates A and E.

Corps of Amboynese Battalion raised following the capture of Amboyna in the Dutch East Indies (now Indonesia). It had a British captain, a lieutenant, a sergeant-major and a drill sergeant with Amboyese natives providing the 600 privates, 20 corporals, 20 sergeants, 10 drummers, an adjutant and 14 artisans. A 32-man detachment was part of a small British force which captured Fort Orange in Ternate during August 1810. The battalion garrisoned Amboyna until 1816 when the islands were returned to the Dutch and the corps was disbanded.

Croatians Croatia and much of the eastern Adriatic coast were ceded to France by Austria in 1809; so were Croat units, which passed from Austrian to French service. By late 1812 and early 1813 the Croat units were increasingly uneasy and desertion became rampant. In April 1813 proposals to raise a Croat regiment in British pay were forwarded from Lord Bentinck to the Earl of Bathurst, but the idea was not entertained and the unit was never raised as a regiment (PRO, WO 1/659). However, the raising of independent Croat companies was permitted. By August two Croat companies had joined the Royal Corsican Rangers (qv) garrison on Curzola (Korcula) island. They were organised, armed and clothed as the Italian Levies (qv).

As British forces based in the Ionian Islands approached the crumbling French defences of the Adriatic they found unexpected assistance from

Officers of several foreign units which had the same uniform as the 95th Rifles (e.g. the Cape Regiment, and the rifle company of Roll's) wore the hussar-style dress shown in this 1812 print after Goddard. Black shako with folding peak, green plume and cords; green dolman with black collar, cuffs and cords, silver buttons; green pelisse edged with brown fur and trimmed with black cords and silver buttons; crimson light infantry sash with cords; green pantaloons with black decoration, black Hessian boots with black trim and tassel; silver-hilted sabre and black belts.

Croat units posted there. In October 1813 when the British besieged Perasto its Croatian garrison laid down its arms in spite of its French commanders. Old Ragusa surrendered in the same circumstances, on 28 October, as did Stagno on 1 November, Zara on 5 December, Cattaro on 3 January 1814 and finally Ragusa (Dubrovnik), the capital of the French Adriatic provinces, on 28 January. Entire Croat battalions now found themselves with the British. However, they did not formally join the British forces, and went back into Austrian service.

(Edward) Dillon's Regiment (See also MAA 328). With the resumption of war with France in 1803, Dillon's continued to garrison Malta until 1808 when it went to Sicily. Its composition became very mixed with men of some 22 nationalities in its ranks, Italians and Spaniards being the most numerous. While in Malta the regiment showed steady conduct during the repression of the mutiny of Froberg's unit (qv) – another corps made up from various nationalities. In Sicily from the end of 1808, its number increased to some 1,200 all ranks in 1810. Five companies were detached to form part of the force deployed in eastern Spain during 1812. They were united with Roll's (qv) into a provisional battalion which fought at Castalla, Tarragona, Biar and other actions, going up the coast until the Allies reached France in March 1814. A month later hostilities ceased, and Roll-Dillon's provisional battalion was dissolved. The rest of the regiment had been sent to Cartagena, Spain, in early 1813, to relieve de Watteville's. In spite of a decent battle record Dillon's had a serious rate of desertion; nearly 300 men had absconded in 1811-1813, and this may have influenced its not being deployed extensively against the French. Six companies were reviewed 'favourably' at Alicante in May 1813 (PRO, WO 27/120). The various companies of the regiment were concentrated at Gibraltar in 1814, and Dillon's disbanded there in January 1815. *Uniform*: See Plate E.

Dutch Levy Also called Dutch Light Infantry Battalion. Unit formed at Yarmouth from January 1814 with the Dutch former prisoners of war still in England, under the command of Col Pankhurst; the battalion appears to have been about 1,000 strong. It was meant to palliate the 'present want of troops to garrison the Fortresses in Holland', and sailed for Helovetslys shortly thereafter (PRO, WO 1/658).

Uniform: a shipment of 1,000 blue coats with orange facings, along with waistcoats, trousers, gaiters, half-stockings, shoes, shakos with plumes, knapsacks, canteens, greatcoats and camp equipage was consigned for the Dutch Levy raised in England on 22.12.1813 and shipped on 7.2.1814 (PRO, WO 1/888). There were further and larger shipments to Holland in May 1814 of similar uniforms and equipments for 'Dutch Levies', but these were obviously intended for new troops raised in that country and not the initial Dutch Levy raised in England (PRO, WO 1/853).

Foreign Corps of Waggoners Raised from May 1815 in Hanover, led by Dutch with some British officers. Attached to the British Royal Waggon Train, it had four companies of 100 men and 180 horses each to provide transport for the British forces in Flanders. Disbanded in Hanover on 24.7.1816 (PRO, WO 4/719). *Uniform*: See illustration.

Foreign Hussars Also called the Foreign Troop of Light Dragoons. Formed during 1810 in Sicily with men who could ride from various foreign regiments in British service on the island. It usually had around 75 to 85 all ranks, and was attached to the 20th Light Dragoons as an extra troop. In June 1812 it embarked with the 20th for eastern Spain. It was heavily engaged against the French at Ordal, about 35km west of Barcelona, on 13.9.1813, losing 16 casualties in a successful charge with the 20th Light Dragoons and the Brunswick Hussars. The foreign troopers were 'with very few exceptions German' and, following a recommendation which was approved by the Duke of York on 20.12.1813, the troop was amalgamated into the Brunswick Hussars (PRO, WO 1/657).

Foreign Invalids Companies One company of the veterans of Loyal Emigrant (see MAA 328) on the Isle of Wight since 1797, raised to two companies with veterans from Castries and Mortemart's (see MAA 328) from July 1801. Based at Lymington and on the Isle of Wight. Many went back to France with Louis XVIII in May 1814 when the companies were disbanded. Their veterans' pay was maintained by the British government until March 1815. *Uniform:* Red coatee, blue collar and cuffs, men's lace white with a red central line, square-ended and single-spaced, pewter buttons, white breeches, black gaiters, shako with brass plate an white-over-red plume. Officers had gold buttons and lace.

Foreign Recruits Battalion Raised in Cadiz in 1810 from deserters and prisoners, the battalion had a high desertion rate and was not deployed in the field. It received 'much praise' when inspected at Cadiz in May 1813, but 'much wanted' clothing which had 'just arrived' (PRO, WO 27/118 and 120). On 14 November it was converted into the 8th Bn, 60th Foot at Lisbon, and included two rifle companies. In 1814 the battalion went to Gibraltar, where it was disbanded on 31.3.1816, the men being incorporated into the 5th Rifle Bn, 60th Foot (qv). *Uniform:* The clothing which arrived in May 1813 may have been similar to that of the 5/60th, as Capt Charles Leslie mentioned in his journal on 2.12.1813 that the new 8th Bn had caused surprise with 'so many men in green rifle uniform'. Accoutrements were 'partly buff and partly black leather' in May 1813.

Foreign Veterans Company raised at Stade, Germany, in March 1805. Attached to the King's German Legion at Portsmouth in 1806; to Portugal 1808-1813. Ordered expanded into a four-company battalion from 8.12.1812, it had two battalions each of 452 men in 1813, and amalgamated into one battalion of four companies in Flanders in 1814. The corps was disbanded at Hanover on 24.2.1816.

Uniform: Red coatee, blue collar and cuffs, men's lace white with a red central line, square-ended and single-spaced, pewter buttons, white breeches, black gaiters, shako with brass plate and white-over- red plume. Officers had gold buttons and lace.

Froberg's Regiment Raised from May 1804 by Gustave de Montjoie, called Count de Froberg, a rather mysterious French Royalist officer

The Cape Regiment raised from 1806 had, from 1809, a uniform similar to the 95th Rifles which probably looked somewhat like this print by Atkinson. The men were, however, Hottentots, and were armed with muskets instead of rifles. (Anne S.K.Brown Military Collection, Brown University, Providence; photo R.Chartrand)

Officer of the 22nd Foot in the East Indies, c.1812. Round hats were very much in fashion in the East, and the dress of the officers of the Ceylon regiments would have been much the same as this watercolour. (Anne S.K. Brown Military Collection, Brown University, Providence; photo R.Chartrand)

whose true identity remains conjectural. Recruiting was very slow, and the unit only had a lieutenant and ten men on Malta in May 1805. Colonel Froberg concentrated his recruiting efforts in the Balkans; by April 1806 the regiment had 500 men, but this sudden arrival of 'Turks' was not to the liking of the Maltese. Another problem was the lack of officers to command this influx of recruits. A number of mostly Swiss and Germans were commissioned into the corps in autumn 1806. General Villettes posted the regiment to Fort Ricasoli, a rather isolated fortification on the eastern side of the entrance to Valletta harbour. The arrival of 229 Albanians who had been recruited under false pretenses fuelled much resentment, and disaffection secretly spread to Greek recruits. Ringleaders plotted to capture all the officers and use them as hostages to obtain ships and supplies to go back to the Balkans.

On 4.4.1807 the plot was discovered and learning this, 200 Albanians and Greeks mutinied. Some officers were killed, though most escaped but Fort Ricasoli remained in the possession of mutineers holding about 200 loyal officers and men as hostages. General Villettes immediately surrounded the fort with a cordon of loyal troops. On 8 April the mutineers surrendered and marched out; however, in a dramatic move about 20 mutineers – described as the most desperate – ran back into the fort, closed the drawbridge, and fired muskets and artillery. A party of loyal volunteers of Froberg's Reg scaled the walls and secured most of the fort. A few of the surviving mutineers hiding in the fort set fire to the powder magazine on the night of 12 April to create a diversion permitting them to escape. The explosion which created much commotion in Valletta allowed three truly incorrigible characters to escape for few days, but they were caught and quickly executed as were the ringleaders. After this most serious mutiny of any by British troops during the Napoleonic Wars an inquiry uncovered the questionable recruiting methods which had caused such havoc. The authorities were shocked to learn that the men considered themselves kidnapped into British military service. Some 350 men were found to have reasonable grounds for discharge and were repatriated. The regiment was ordered disbanded in June 1807. [2]

---

2 As for Count Froberg, he had previously left Malta to recruit in Istambul. There he ran out of money, borrowed more from the British embassy, then disappeared. He met his end in a skirmish with French cavalry in East Prussia on 10.6.1807 while travelling to the Russian army's headquarters, apparently to offer his services.

Uniform: White cotton jackets and trousers were issued to the men. Whether this or some other dress was 'the uniform of 'roberg' known to a Maltese priest assailed by one of the mutineers remains a moot point. The men were allowed to grow moustaches and hair in their native style.

Greek Light Infantry, 1st Regiment Raised in the Ionian Islands in March 1810 by Capt Richard Church as a single battalion of Greeks and Albanians. It immediately participated in the capture of Santa Maura (Leucadia) from 22 March to 16 April 1810, a sharp affair in which Church was badly wounded. Noted as having 548 officers and men at the time, the corps was later 800 strong and stationed on the island of Zante. The regiment was put on the British establishment from 25.2.1811 with BrigGen Robert Oswald as colonel, and was to have ten companies totalling 1,129 all ranks; it was designated 'The Duke of York's' in 1812. The unit helped quell an insurrection in Montenegro in June 1812; but displayed a 'degree of unwillingness' to embark for Sicily in early 1813. When reviewed there on 22.5.1813 the corps was reported in a 'very indifferent state', with no field officer present in the last ten months; company officers thus found themselves with 'no authority to install good discipline'. A 250-strong detachment was part of the British forces in the expedition against Spezzia and Genoa in March-April 1814. The unit was disbanded on 24.5.1816 (PRO, WO 26/42 and WO 27/120).

The Foreign Corps of Waggoners of 1815-16 had the same uniform as the British Royal Waggon Train shown in this C.H.Smith print. The enlisted men had a red jacket with blue collar and cuffs edged with white, three rows of pewter buttons on the breast, blue or grey-blue pantaloons, black boots or short gaiters, shako with white cords, white-over-red plume and small white metal badge, and black accoutrements. The officers wore scarlet faced with blue with white turnbacks and silver buttons. The front, not visible in this plate, had three rows of buttons with silver cord frames instead of lapels. (Anne S.K.Brown Military Collection, Brown University, Providence; photo R.Chartrand)

Map of the Ionian Islands at the time of the Napoleonic Wars - the theatre of operations for some of the more exotic foreign units in British pay.

Uniform: Reported as wearing Albanian dress in 1810. Lord Byron, who travelled to the area at the time, wrote of 'The wild Albanian kirtled to his knee, with shawl-girt head and ornamented gun, And gold-embroid'rd garments, fair to see' (*Childe Harold*, canto II, LVIII). The orders stipulated that 'clothing and accoutrements were to be made in the Albanian fashion'. The oriental-style jacket was red with yellow cuffs, the facing colour, and yellow trim ornamenting the jacket – gold for the Greek officers – with a white *fustanella* or Greek kilt, breeches and stockings, sandals with ties, white shirt and small cap (see illustrations). They would not wear knapsacks, only haversacks; and by March 1813 preferred the standard British musket to a sort of cut-down weapon they initially carried. They were also supposed to have pistols but, as they were always rather volatile, it was 'thought prudent' not to issue these. The corps had 'a fancy pair of small colours and not according to regulation' in 1813 (PRO, WO 1/313 and WO 27/118).

Greek Light Infantry, 2nd Regiment Raised from 29.6.1813 by Sir Richard Church, to have 454 all ranks in four companies plus staff. As in the 1st Greek Light Infantry, the officers were all Greeks except for the British regimental staff. The unit took part in the capture of the island of Paxos during 1814, but was disbanded that October.

Uniform: Basically as the 1st, the red jacket having green regimental facings at the cuffs and trimmings; a red skull cap had a green turn-up and pompon. C.H.Smith's print shows men of this unit armed with Baker rifles and braces of pistols; however we have found no evidence of this weapon being sent in numbers to troops in Sicily and the Ionian Islands. (Nor – se above – was it thought wise to issue the pistols.) The most likely armament was the standard India pattern musket with its bayonet. See illustration and Plate D.

Independent Companies of Foreigners See MAA 319 *British Forces in North America 1793-1815*.

Ionian Islands Volunteer Militias In early October 1809 the Ionian Islands of Zante, Cephalonia, Ithaca and Cerigo were taken by a British force. Headquarters were set up on Zante, the most important island, and Maj J.H.Slessor, 35th Foot, became governor and commandant of the Zante island militia – which he described as 'near 2,000 men, a kind of volunteer force, armed at their own expense'. By 1810 a force of some 4,000 militiamen was reported, some enlisting into Oswald's 1st Greek Light Infantry Regiment (qv).

Italian Levy Also called the Italian Regiments. Following a request by the Marquis of Wellesley to form a corps from among Italian prisoners of war hostile to Napoleon's rule – many having been drafted into the Imperial army by force – they were assembled in England from October 1811, and sent to Malta under the command of LtCol J.Burke. On 13.5.1812 Lord William Bentinck issued at Palermo, Sicily, a detailed 'Regulation for the formation of an Italian Levy to be raised for His Majesty's Service'. The establishment of each regiment was one lieutenant-colonel, two majors, eight captains, 16 lieutenants, eight ensigns, five staff officers, five staff sergeants, a drum-major, 32 sergeants, 32 corporals, 32 carabiniers, 18 drummers, and 1,136 privates – a total of 1,296 officers and men. Each regiment was divided into two battalions each having four companies. Each company had four officers, three sergeants, four corporals, four carabiniers (elite soldiers), two drummers and 142 privates; the 1st and 5th companies had an extra drummer serving as a fifer.

During May 1812 Burke's recruits went from Malta to Iccacia, Sicily, and were there formed into the 1st Italian Regiment. In late May the 2nd Italian Regt was raised under Capt Grant (formerly of the HEIC army and a relative of Lord Bentinck) and stationed at Cerini, near Palermo. The 1st Italian Regt had mostly Austrian officers while the 2nd had 'principally Piedmontese, Swiss and Austrians ... many of them very respectable', according to Lord Bentinck. Some 1,157 men of the Estero Infantry Regt of the Kingdom of the Two Sicilies were also incorporated into the levy. A 3rd Italian Regt was organised towards the end of 1813 from 'a further levy' amongst Italian prisoners of war in Britain. All three regiments were recruited up to or over the establishment. A 4th Regt is sometimes mentioned but was not actually raised.

The 2nd Regt embarked some 1,200 strong at Palermo for eastern Spain in November 1812. It lost nearly 140 men through desertion in early 1813; there were also a few traitors in the ranks, who plotted to turn

Greek officer and soldiers, c.1810-1820. (Contemporary print)

over villages near Alicante to the French in February. Informers leaked the plot to Gen Whittingham, who had the ringleaders arrested and executed. The 2nd was then disarmed and sent back to Alicante. It seems that LtCol Grant was an ineffectual commander whose sneering manner made him detested by his men. The 2nd was reinstated when its members gave their word to serve honourably. Sadly, historians seem to have retained only this one unit's bad conduct condemning the whole Italian Levy as bad troops. Closer scrutiny reveals this to be an over-hasty conclusion.

The 1st Regt embarked for eastern Spain in December 1812 with 40 officers and 1,153 men. Lieutenant-Colonel Burke was a good commander and the regiment was accordingly steadier. It later went into action against superior French forces at Biar – one of the finest rearguard actions by the British in the Peninsular War, according to Oman. At Castalla on 12-13.4.1813 – where Marshal Suchet's advance on Alicante was halted – the regiment was heavily engaged. A detachment, probably from men left in Sicily, was at the siege and capture of Trieste in October 1813. In April 1814 both Italian regiments sailed from Tarragona and joined other troops from Sicily led by Bentinck, which included the 3rd Italian Regiment. Some 1,220 men from the three regiments took part in the siege and capture of Genoa from 13 to 17 April.

On the whole the Italian regiments were considered good by the British military authorities. In September 1815, as the time was approaching to reduce the corps, a senior War Office official concluded that they 'have conducted themselves in the most exemplary manner and on the few occasions where they have been employed against the enemy, they have done themselves great credit, particularly in the attack on Genoa' (PRO, WO 6/175).

Uniform: Bentinck strove to make a 'total distinction' between these corps and other units, and thus 'dressed them in blue'. See the text of Plate H for the regulation. In a manuscript addition to his 1814 uniform chart (in the example at the Bibliothèque Nationale in Paris) Hamilton Smith confirms this dress, showing a plain blue coatee with red collar and cuffs and grey pantaloons. Each NCO and private was to receive every second year a cloth jacket, a pair of cloth pantaloons, a pair of cloth half-gaiters, a shako with tuft, a fatigue cap, a white cotton or linen jacket, a pair of white cotton or linen pantaloons, a pair of white cotton or linen half-gaiters, three shirts, two pairs of shoes, two pairs of soles, a leather stock, and a set of comb and brushes; he was to receive a greatcoat every three years, and a 'fatigue dress when required only'.

Recruits sent from England to Sicily in late 1813 were each issued for the crossing with a white cloth jacket, a pair of pantaloons, a leather cap, shirts, stockings, stocks and clasps, a canvas frock, a pair of canvas trousers and a haversack (PRO, WO 1/311 and WO 6/174).

Java Volunteers or Hussars Also called the Java Light Cavalry Regiment. Following the capture of the Dutch East Indies (Indonesia) by Anglo-Indian forces in 1811, two cavalry squadrons were organised in India during 1812 to serve on the island of Java under Capt L.H.O'Brien of the Honourable East India Company Madras cavalry, with Indian volunteers from the HEIC's forces. It arrived in Java in early 1813; served mostly in Batavia (Djakarta); and was disbanded in 1816 when Java was handed back to Holland. *Uniform*: See illustration.

King's German Legion See MAA 206 *The Hanoverian Army 1792-1816*; also MAA 338 & 339, *The King's German Legion (1) & (2)*, publication March & May 2000.

Malta Coast Artillery Corps raised from 1800 to help man the various batteries in Malta, especially at Valletta. It had two companies and its status appears to have been an embodied militia. Ordered disbanded on 16.2.1815. *Uniform*: Initially a cotton fatigue jacket and cotton trousers, blue sash at waist and round hat. Later the same as the British Royal Artillery.

Maltese Military Artificers Two companies of 78 men each raised from January 1806 for service in Malta. A third 'war company' was raised for service elsewhere in the Mediterranean and served at Gibraltar. The corps had Maltese NCOs and men and was led by officers of the Royal Engineers except for a Maltese adjutant; in all it numbered 276 including staff. Disbanded in 1817. *Uniform*: See Plate C and illustrations.

Maltese Police Corps A para-military body of about 224 'police' was on the local establishment of the fortress island and subject to the military authority of the Inspector of Maltese Corps. Disbanded in February 1815. *Uniform*: In September 1812 the Inspector, LtCol Vivian,

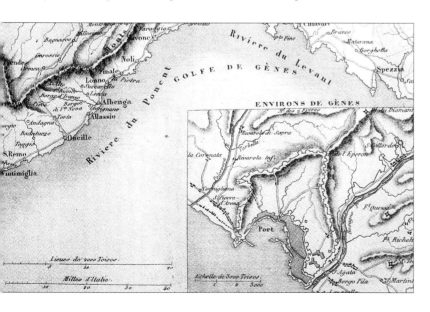

Map of Genoa, c.1800-1815. The capture of this port in April 1814 was the last major action involving Britain's foreign units in the Mediterranean. The Italian Levy regiments and the Greek Light Infantry both distinguished themselves in the capture of the outer works which led to the city's surrender.

ordered for the unit from England a supply of grey cloth jackets and pantaloons, black cloth gaiters, white kersey waistcoats, black felt shakos with cockades, brass plates and 184 red and white tufts, plus 40 red and white plumes for sergeants (PRO, WO 6/174).

Maltese Provincial Battalions Two single-battalion 'regiments' raised for garrison duty on the island from November 1802. Officers and men were Maltese, the 1st Bn under the Marquis Parisi, the 2nd led by Count Gatto. The initial establishment called for 1,000 men in ten companies, but reduced to a more realistic 700 per battalion. In late 1806 both battalions were described as in a 'reduced and mutilated state', and were amalgamated into a single battalion of 918 officers and men to render them 'much more efficient and serviceable' and to act as a recruiting depot (PRO, CO 158/3 and WO 1/667). The battalion was ordered disbanded on 16.2.1815. *Uniform*: See Plate C.

Maltese Veteran Battalion A four-company battalion of 300 older soldiers was formed on the local establishments from about 1803. Most were veterans of the small army of the Knights of Malta. Their main duties were to provide guards and act in aid of civil power. Ordered disbanded on 16 February 1815. *Uniform*: Grey faced with red. The officers had silver buttons and lace.

Meuron (See also MAA 328). This Swiss regiment remained in garrison at Seringapatam, India, until 1806, when a cadre of 35 officers and 132 men were sent back to Europe; the remainder were sent to the Mediterranean in 1807. The unit was stationed successively at Gibraltar, in Sicily and finally in Malta until 1813, when its strength stood at 1,339 men. Sent to Canada during the War of 1812, it arrived at Quebec in August 1813. It went to the area south of Montreal and was posted at La Prairie and Forts Chambly, St Jean and Île-aux-Noix near the US border until September 1814 when, as part of Sir George Prevost's 10,000-man army, it marched on the American town of Plattsburg. Meuron's lost 14 men in this bungled operation, and after six days Prevost withdrew. Meuron's went back to various posts in Montreal. In mid-1816 the regiment was ordered disbanded, the officers and men being offered land grants; 35

A trooper of the Java Volunteers or Hussars is shown on foot in this 1815 print by C.H.Smith. He wears a blue dolman faced with yellow at collar and cuffs and trimmed with white lace and cords with pewter buttons; his red (turban?) headdress is trimmed with white, and he wears white pantaloons. The mounted troopers belong to, left, the Governor-General's Body Guard, in scarlet faced with blue; and right, the Bengal Light Cavalry in light blue faced with red. Both show white cords, and a blue headdress trimmed white. (Anne S.K.Brown Military Collection, Brown University, Providence; photo R.Chartrand)

SOUTHERN ITALY
1: Private, Watteville's Swiss Regt, 1803
2: Private, Chasseurs Britanniques, c.1806-09
3: Bugler, Royal Corsican Rangers, c.1808

P. Courcelle

AFRICA
1: Private, Cape Regiment, 1806-08
2: Drummer, Royal African Corps, c.1810
3: Officer, Royal African Corps, 1808

F. Courcelle

B

MALTA
1: Sergeant, Maltese Military Artificers, 1808-15
2: Officer, 1st Malta Provincial Bn, 1802-06
3: Drummer, Royal Regt of Malta, 1805-11

P. Courcelle

1

2

3

C

2

3

1

D

PORTUGAL & SPAIN
1: Field officer, Chasseurs Britanniques, c.1810-14
2: Sergeant, Dillon's Regiment, 1813-14
3: Drummer, Roll's Swiss Regiment, 1813-1814

P. Courcelle

1

2

3

E

P. Courcelle

1　　　　2　　　　3

F

CANADA 1813-16
1: Officer with colours, Meuron's Swiss Regt
2: Fusilier, Meuron's Swiss Regt
3: Officer, Light Company, Watteville's Swiss Regt

ITALIAN UNITS
1: Carabinier, Italian Levy, 1812-15
2: Captain, Italian Levy, 1812-15
3: Fusilier, Piedmontese Legion, 1814

P. Courcelle

remained in Canada, the others leaving Quebec on 26 July and the final disbandment taking place at Harwich on 24 September. *Uniform*: See Plate G.

However, the military role of Meuron's men in Canada did not quite end there. Since its establishment in 1811 Lord Selkirk's Scottish colony on the shores of the Red River (now the area of Winnipeg, Manitoba) had been threatened by fur traders supported by the powerful North West Company, who did not want settlers in this territory. To protect the area Lord Selkirk hired privately a force of four officers and 106 veterans – 90 from Meuron's and ten from Wateville's (qv). Leaving Montreal on 4.6.1816, they learned on the way that the colony had been attacked and destroyed. The Swiss remained at Fort William (Thunder Bay, Ontario) but a detachment of 30 men went to the Red River area; on 10.1.1817 they took Fort Douglas and arrested the suspect fur traders. The rest of the Swiss contingent joined them in June, and many stayed as settlers.

Minorca Regiment (Queen's Own Germans, 97th Foot) Raised from late 1798, this infantry regiment was renamed the 'Queen's Own Germans' in 1802 (see MAA 328). On 28.1.1805 the unit was taken into the British line as the '97th (Queen's Own German) Regiment of Foot'. It was becoming less foreign as more British recruits were accepted into it, and was no longer considered a foreign corps after 1810. In 1808 the 97th was sent to Portugal and fought at Vimiero (21.9.1808), going on to Porto, Talavera de la Reina (7.7.1809), Busaco (27.9.1810), the first siege of Badajos (February-March 1811) and Albuera (14 April). By then its strength of 900 was reduced to about 300 men. It was transferred to Ireland in October 1811 to recruit. It embarked for Canada in 1814, and was engaged against the Americans during the siege of Fort Erie in September. Returning to Britain in 1815, it was disbanded at Limerick on 10.12.1818.

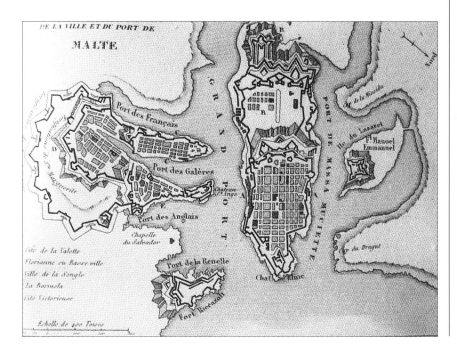

Map of Valetta, Malta, 1800-1815. The harbour city's formidable fortifications were manned by various Maltese units as well as British and other foreign regiments. At lower left is Fort Ricasoli, scene of the violent mutiny by Froberg's regiment in April 1807.

Sir Hudson Lowe, commander of the Royal Corsican Rangers, c.1815. A fine regimental commander, Lowe was to be remembered by history as Napoleon's jailer on St Helena from 1815 to the Emperor's death in 1821. Lowe was not blessed with a particularly flexible character - as the portrait suggests - and this earned him vilification at the hands of historians sympathetic to Napoleon. The uniform is somewhat uncertain in this print after Frémy.

Uniform: According to De Bosset's 1803 chart, a red coatee with yellow collar and cuffs, white turnbacks, white lace with a black line, square-ended and set equally, pewter buttons, white breeches and stovepipe shako. Silver lace and buttons for officers. In 1805 the facing colour was changed to blue, the officers' lace and buttons to gold. In Pearse's tailoring notes of c.1808-1810 the men's lace was white with a blue central line and a yellow line on each side, set evenly and square-ended. Grey pantaloons, short grey gaiters and the 'Belgic' shako were taken into wear from 1812-13. According to C.H.Smith's chart of 1814 the men's lace now had a yellow and a blue line and was set in pairs. Drummers' coatees were, according to Pearse, red with blue cuffs and collar and had 15 yards of broad lace, 14 yards of looping lace (the same as the men), 3 yards of fringes, the broad lace set at the 'seams, body frames down the sleeve 2 darts'. The broad lace was white, an inch wide with a central blue line and a yellow line on each side, each line one-fifth of an inch wide.

Piedmontese Legion Organised at Colchester in early 1814 following an agreement of 3 February between Lord Bathurst and Count St Martin d'Aglie, its commander. It was to have about 3,000 all ranks recruited from Italian prisoners of war interned in Britain, and was for the service of the King of Sardinia in the Mediterranean, although initially paid and equipped by Britain and having some British officers attached to help in its organisation. By June two small battalions each of six 100-man companies were reported formed, and there was even hope of having a 28-strong band of music. News of the end of the war in Europe brought further recruiting to a standstill; another difficulty was the lack of sufficient numbers of Italian officers among the prisoners. In any event the battalions embarked for the Mediterranean and reached Genoa on 12 September, passing into Piedmontese service four days later (PRO, WO 1/659). *Uniform*: See Plate H.

Roll Swiss regiment raised from December 1794 by the Baron de Roll for British service (see also MAA 328). Following its service in Egypt in 1801-03 the regiment was based in Gibraltar from June 1803 to November 1806, when it transferred to Sicily. It took part in a few skirmishes against the French in Calabria and Puglia, recruiting 150 Germans and Poles from the prisoners. In 1807 the corps took part in the unsuccessful expedition against Egypt, losing three companies to the Turco-Egyptians at Rosetta; the main body fought admirably and kept the enemy at bay during the retreat. Back in Sicily, Roll's flank companies took part in the capture of the islands of Ischia and Prosida off the southern coast of Italy. In 1809 over 400 officers and men from the 4th Swiss Regt in French service, captured by the British in Portugal, joined Roll. In March 1810 the regiment stood at 12 companies including a grenadier, a chasseur or light infantry and a rifle company. Two companies (160 men) participated with distinction in the capture of Santa Maura (Leucadia) from 22 March to 16 April 1810. In September 1810 the light company took part in the repulse of Murat, the former marshal named King of Naples, who attacked near Messina in Sicily.

In 1812 three companies went to Malta and two to the Ionian Islands, others were in Sicily, and declared 'generally favourable' at an inspection in May 1813 (PRO, WO 27/120). Four companies were detached to the

Anglo-Sicilian force in eastern Spain, forming a provisional battalion with Dillon's Regiment (qv), and were joined by four more at Alicante in August. The temporary Roll-Dillon battalion saw much action, distinguishing itself at Alicante, Castala, Tarragona and Biar. After hostilities ceased in April 1814 Roll-Dillon's was dissolved and the companies of Roll returned to Sicily.

The regiment's services were not quite over. In the spring of 1815 the chasseurs and two fusilier companies were part of a force which finally toppled Murat from the throne of Naples. With the final exile of Napoleon that summer Sicily was once again part of the Kingdom of Naples; in October the British evacuated the island, and Roll's went to the Ionian Islands until August 1816. It was disbanded in Venice on 24.8.1816; these admirable Swiss soldiers then marched home to Switzerland, unarmed but in disciplined order, and were greeted by their countrymen at Lake Constance with homecoming ceremonies.

Uniform: See also MAA 328. The red coatee had sky blue collar and cuffs, white turnbacks, white lace with a sky blue line set in pairs, and pewter buttons; white breeches, stovepipe shako. In about 1803-05 the shape of the regimental lace, which was pointed, was transformed by the addition of a false tassel at the point of each loop. This was in honour of the Swiss Guards of the former French royal household troops, which had such loopings. The facing colour changed to a darker shade of sky blue at this time, resembling royal blue. The elite companies had wings in the dark sky blue facing colour instead of the usual red, trimmed with regimental lace. Grey pantaloons, short grey gaiters and the 'Belgic' shako were taken into wear from 1812; the shako plate had a sphinx badge below the cipher GR and, from about 1815, 'Peninsula' above. See Plate C for drummers, and the illustration of LtCol Bosset on page 47 for officers. The rifle company's uniform was patterned after the 95th Rifles.

Royal African Corps While nearly all officers were British the corps' last commander, LtCol Charles Macarthy, was a French émigré of Irish descent. It was initially recruited from Britons condemned as incorrigible and sent to the deadly climate of the West African coast rather than to the gallows; but by 1807 foreigners already numbered 108 out of the corps' 265 NCOs and men. By 1809 there were 102 British and 94 European foreigners. Blacks were enlisted into the corps from 1805, when 200 were transferred from the disbanded York Rangers (qv). In 1813 there were about 475 black soldiers filling five companies; most black recruits were obtained from the Liberated Africans Yard at Sierra Leone.

The Maltese Military Artificers at Gibraltar had a similar uniform to these Royal Military Artificers, shown between 1802 and 1812. At left, a private; centre, a sergeant distinguished by his crimson sash with a central black stripe, yellow epaulette, and halberd or half-pike; at right, a corporal with yellow epaulette. Chevrons, three for sergeants and two for corporals, replaced epaulettes from 1802. Blue coatee with black collar, cuffs and shoulder straps, white turnbacks, yellow lace, brass buttons; white breeches, black gaiters, stovepipe shako with brass plate and white plume. This 1855 print after Connolly is generally accurate, except that there was no loop at the collar and no inside turnback at the coat skirts.

Officer, Royal Engineers, 1802. British engineers supervised foreign units of artificers, especially in Malta and Gibraltar. Until 1813 they wore blue faced with black, gold buttons and epaulettes; crimson sash; white breeches with boots, and a bicorn hat with a white plume. The artificer units wore the same uniform colours. (C.C.P.Lawson after Loftie; Anne S.K.Brown Military Collection, Brown University, Providence; photo R.Chartrand)

First named 'Fraser's Corps of Infantry' after its commander LtCol John Fraser, the corps arrived in Goree during January 1801. In November 1801 the detachment at Sierra Leone repulsed an attack by natives. It was a small unit, having only 98 all ranks at Goree and 59 in Sierra Leone in August 1803. On 18.1.1804 Goree was captured by a French naval force after fierce resistance by Fraser and his men. However, on 9 March, the small French garrison in Goree surrendered without resistance to HMS *Inconstant*, which returned with 230 men of the renamed 'Royal African Corps' on 25 April. In 1805 Lt J.Martyn and 35 men volunteered to take part in Capt Mungo Parks' exploration of the interior up the Niger river; nearly all perished. In July 1809 a force of 166 officers and men took part in the capture of the French fort of St Louis in Senegal. In March 1814 some 150 men of the corps went up the river Pongo to destroy slave-trading stations.

The 1800 African Corps had two companies augmented to seven in May-June 1803 and ten from 25.3.1804, but six companies were in England and were sent to the West Indies in October. Raised to 12 companies from 25.3.1805, the corps was divided on 25.10.1806 into two units: the Royal African Corps for Africa, and the Royal West India Rangers for the West Indies, each to have eight companies of 100 men each. On 24.8.1807 the Royal African Corps was retitled Royal York Rangers, and raised to ten companies in September. It was again split into two units on 25.6.1808: the Royal York Rangers, which went to the West Indies, and the recreated Royal African Corps, with four companies posted in Africa. It was enlarged to six companies on 25.8.1808, and to eight from 25.8.1809, of which three were at Goree, three at Senegal, one at Sierra Leone, and one as a depot in Guernsey. It was raised to 11 companies during 1811, ten serving in Africa, and reduced to ten (including three black companies) from February 1817.

Mortality was always very high for white troops in West Africa, and it was finally decided to garrison these small possessions with black troops only; the six companies of Europeans were transferred to the Cape. On 24.6.1819 the four black companies in West Africa were disbanded, followed on 24.6.1821 by the six European companies at Cape Town.

Uniform: Initially red coatee, green collar and cuffs, white turnbacks, white lace, pewter buttons. Facings changed to blue from April 1804 when the corps became 'Royal'. Pearse's notes of c.1808-1810 specify the privates' red coatee to have square-ended, evenly-spaced lace with red and blue central line. C.H.Smith's chart shows the square-ended lace in pairs with a brown (red?

nd a blue line. The regimental badge approved n September 1804 was a ion and crown (PRO, WO 3/336). Some allowances were made for the tropical climate; in December 1800 'white hats' were ordered issued instead of the usual forage caps. In March 1805 each soldier of the detachment with Mungo Parks' expedition was provided with a large cloak, a white hat, two flannel vests, two pairs of trousers, leather gaiters and shoes. It would seem that, for ordinary duties, the men mostly wore white linen jackets, probably with blue collar and cuffs, white trousers and white hats, shakos and red coatees being kept for formal occasions. Black accoutrements were noted as being in wear for 19 years in an 1821 request for replacements (PRO, WO 27/90 and WO 43/149). See also Plate B.

A field officer of the Royal Engineers and a private of the Royal Sappers and Miners, 1814. The dress of the 'war company'of Maltese Military Artificers at Gibraltar from 1813 was the same as that shown for the Royal Sappers and Miners: red faced with blue, trimmed with yellow lace, brass buttons; grey pantaloons and gaiters; Belgic shako with brass plate, white plume and yellow cords. Officers of the Royal Engineers supervised the artificers and sappers. They wore scarlet with blue collar, cuffs and lapels, white turnbacks, gold buttons, epaulettes and lace; crimson sash; grey pantaloons with red stripe; and a black bicorn with a white plume. (Print after C.H.Smith; Anne S.K.Brown Military Collection, Brown University, Providence; photo R.Chartrand)

Royal Corsican Rangers Raised in Malta from 14.9.1803 and commanded by Hudson Lowe, to have ten companies of 60 men each with mostly Corsican officers. It formed part of the British expedition to assist Naples in November 1805, but the force was evacuated in February 1806 as 40,000 French invaded southern Italy, the Rangers withdrawing into Calabria with the Neapolitan army. The unit took part in the battle of Maida (4.7.1806) where Gen Reynier's French army was defeated by Gen Sir John Stuart's Anglo-Italian force; and fought in the capture of Monteleone and the siege of Scilla (7-23 July). It was sent to Capri in September. In October 1808 the French attacked Capri, which capitulated with the honours of war on the 16th, its garrison transferring to Sicily on the 26th. Some 442 men of the corps took part in the capture of the island of Ischia near Naples, 24-26.7.1809. Two companies served with the British force which captured the Ionian Islands of Zante, Cephallonia, Ithaca and Cerigo without resistance, 2-16.10.1809. Two companies participated in the capture of Santa Maura (Leucadia), 22.3.-16.4.1810.

Augmented to 12 companies in December 1811, the Rangers were posted in the Ionian Islands, with detachments at Lissa from 1812 and at the capture and garrisoning of Lagosta (Lastovo) and Curzola (Korcula)

Working dress of the Royal Sappers and Miners, 1813; the Maltese Military Artificers at Gibraltar would have had a similar uniform. Red jacket with blue collar and cuffs, brass buttons; grey pantaloons with red stripe; black cap with brass corps initials. (Print after Connolly)

from early 1813. A detachment took part in the siege and capture of Trieste in October 1813 and Ragusa (Dubrovnik) in December 1813-January 1814. The regiment was at the siege and capture of Genoa in April 1814; it then returned to the Ionian Islands, and was disbanded on Corfu (occupied by the British 26.4.1814) on 24.9.1816. *Uniform*: See Plate A.

Royal Foreign Artillery. See MAA 294 *British Forces in the West Indies 1793-1815*.

Royal Regiment of Malta. Initially to be raised as a two-battalion corps from 1805, the establishment was reduced to one battalion of 750 men in 1806. Sent to Capri, the regiment participated in its defence against the successful French attacks of 4-5.10.1808, losing 25 killed and wounded and some 680 taken prisoner including 22 officers. However, the remaining part of the regiment managed to save the colours and get back to the ships. The remnant, about 300 strong, was then deployed for the raid on Naples, in which abortive operation the regiment lost its colours. No doubt as an encouragement, new colours were presented in 1809. However, the establishment was reduced to 400 men in 1810, and the unit was ordered disbanded on 30.4.1811.

Uniform: Red coatee, blue collar and cuffs, white turnbacks, white lace with a blue line square-ended and set evenly, pewter buttons, white breeches, shako. Gold buttons and lace for officers. For drummers, see Plate C.

Royal West India Rangers See MAA 294 *British Forces in the West Indies 1793-1815*.

Royal York Rangers See MAA 294 *British Forces in the West Indies 1793-1815*.

Sicilian Regiment Raised in Sicily from May 1806 as a light infantry battalion of 500 men by MajGen Sir John Stuart, it was part of his force at Maida on 4 July although, barely raised and disciplined, it was held in reserve. Back in Sicily it was enlarged to ten companies. Some 24 officers and 548 men took part in the unsuccessful expedition to Egypt in March 1807; they seem to have been held in reserve, as the unit had only seven killed and ten wounded at Alexandria, and was evacuated on 19 September. Two more companies were added in 1808. Each company had four officers, six sergeants, five corporals, four acting corporals, an artisan, ten carabiniers (elite sharpshooters apparently armed with rifles, since they had sword bayonets), two buglers and 68 privates – a total of 100 officers and men. While in Malta the regiment was presented with colours on 2.3.1809. It was later stationed in Sicily until disbanded on 4.1816 [3]. *Uniform*: See Plate D.

---

3 This unit has sometimes been mentioned as serving with the British forces in eastern Spain from 1812 and at Genoa in 1814. This is a confusion with the contingent of Italian troops from the Kingdom of the Two Sicilies. The French had taken Naples and set it up as a puppet kingdom, but the legitimate Bourbon king, Ferdinando IV, had retreated to Sicily with part of his army, which served with the British. For details and uniforms, see Giancarlo Boeri & Piero Crociani, *L'Esercito Borbonico dal 1789 al 1815*, Rome, 1989.

Sicilian Volunteers In early 1807 an attempt was made to attach an additional Sicilian company to each British regiment in Sicily. Some Sicilians were enlisted, but only the 20th Foot had recruited as many as half of its company by March 1807, the 21st having only 14 recruits. The scheme failed through lack of interest by regimental commanders (PRO, WO 1/303). Eventually British regiments that went back to England transferred such recruits to the unit of Sicilian Volunteers formed to gather them from January 1808 on the Isle of Wight. They were repatriated and drafted into other Italian units in 1813.

Spanish Volunteers A shortage of replacements from Britain for Wellington's army in Spain eventually made it necessary 'to incorporate some of the Spaniards' in British regiments during early 1812. A General Order of 18.5.1812 authorised regiments to have up to 100 'Spanish Volunteers'; they were to be at least 5ft 6ins tall and aged between 19 and 27 years. They took an oath to serve for the duration of the war in the Peninsula; could freely attend Roman Catholic services; would 'be fed, and clothed, and paid in the same manner as the other soldiers; and ... posted to companies indiscriminately, as any other recruits would be'. Instead of bounty money they received 'a knapsack, two pairs of shoes, and two shirts'. Anticipating a culture shock for the Spaniards, Wellington further specified that they were to be treated 'with the utmost kindness and indulgence, and brought by degrees to the system of discipline of the [British] army'.

Naturally, everyone anticipated many difficulties with such a measure. However, the famous Spanish guerrilla leader Don Julian Sanchez had a high regard for Wellington and set about finding recruits. Soon, Rifleman Costello of the 95th related that 'we found ... to our surprise, [that] we were joined by a sufficient number of Spaniards to give ten or twelve men to each company in the battalion'. The new recruits had been given 'but three alternatives to choose from, to enter the British [service], Don Julian's service or be hanged!' – so they 'gladly joined the British regiments. Many of them were even made corporals, and, indeed, proved themselves worthy of their new comrades, whom they rivaled in every undertaking of courage and determination.' Costello further noted that 'the gallantry of the Spaniards in our regiment makes me believe, had those countrymen during the war been properly commanded, they would have made excellent soldiers.' These volunteers received the uniform, equipment and weapons of the British regiment in which they served.

Surinam Chasseurs See MAA 294 *British Forces in the West Indies 1793-1815.*

Watteville (See also MAA 328). The year 1803 found this Swiss regiment in Egypt until March, when it transferred to Malta. On 22.11.1805 Watteville's landed near Naples as part of the Anglo-Russian attempt to protect the Kingdom of the Two Sicilies from the French; but they were forced to evacuate in January 1806 as 40,000 men under Marshal Masséna arrived and Napoleon's brother Joseph was proclaimed king on 30 April. The British forces, including Watteville's, regrouped in Sicily from February 1806 under Gen Sir John Stuart. The energetic Stuart decided to attack the French contingent under Gen Reynier in Calabria; his 5,300 men, which included Watteville's, utterly defeated Reynier's 7,000 men at Maida on 4.7.1806, inflicting casualties of 500

Peter Lardy von Nevenburg (1757-1818), an officer in Meuron's Swiss Regiment, c.1810. (Print after portrait)

This Regimental colour of Roll's Swiss Regiment is, curiously, yellow instead of the bright blue of its regimental facings. A possible explanation is that it was carried by the combined Roll-Dillon battalion which served in eastern Spain during 1812-1814. Yellow was the facing colour of Dillon's; but the devices, including the Masonic eye symbol and the motto on the garter - *'schwebe uber uns uns segne unsere treue'* - were those of Roll's.

killed, 800 wounded and 1,100 prisoners. Watteville's went back to Melazzo, Sicily, and thence to Gibraltar in December 1807 before returning to Sicily in April 1808. Over 600 of the corps took part in the capture of Ischia and Scilla on 24-30.6.1809.

By 1810 the origins of the men in the ranks were extremely varied, consisting of 231 Germans, 156 Swiss, 120 Italians, 40 French, 39 Greeks, 238 Poles, Hungarians and Russians, and 10 Dutchmen. The 42 officers were Swiss except for three Frenchmen and

Fort Erie, Upper Canada (now Ontario), was the scene in August and September 1814 of desperate fighting which caused Watteville's Regiment heavy casualties. The former Minorca Regiment or Queen's Own Germans, which became the 97th Foot, was also engaged at Fort Erie.

four Germans. The band had 14 musicians apparently paid for by the officers.

Detachments were involved in small raids on the coast of Calabria and in the repulse of Murat's attempt to invade Sicily at San Placido on 18.9.1810. Many of the Slav soldiers taken prisoner enlisted in Watteville's, bringing it up to 1,410 men; an 11th company was organised. The regiment landed in October 1811 at Cadiz, then under siege by the French, to reinforce its garrison. In November a 12th company was formed from French deserters. The corps did not see any heavy action and remained in Cadiz into 1813. Five companies were detached to Cartagena between January 1812 and March 1813.

In March 1813 the regiment was ordered to Canada, and arrived at Quebec on 6 June. It immediately boarded small boats for Montreal and on to Kingston (Upper Canada, now Ontario). The two flank companies, left behind and now rejoining the regiment, were captured when their transport was taken by an American ship about 30 miles from Kingston on 5 October. On 6.5.1814 six companies (including two newly formed flank companies) participated in the capture of Oswego (New York state). Watteville's went on to join Gen Drummond's army in the Niagara peninsula and was involved in the siege of Fort Erie. On 15 August the corps suffered heavily during an assault at Snake Hill near the fort; some 83 men literally disappeared when a mine blew up, besides another 24 killed and 27 wounded. Two days later the Americans made a vigorous sortie which partly destroyed Watteville's, some 278 officers and men being wounded and made prisoner in the engagement. The compromised siege was lifted; Watteville's was made the scapegoat, but it seems in retrospect that it was unlucky rather than cowardly, having to face overwhelming odds. Watteville's spent the winter on the Niagara with Drummond's army. After news of the end of hostilities reached the unit on 20.2.1815 it went to garrison Kingston in April. In June 1816 it was ordered to Quebec, and was disbanded there on 24 October. Although offered land grants to stay as settlers, most officers and men went back to Europe; however, a few enlisted in the service of Lord Selkirk and went to the Red River. *Uniform*: See Plates A and G.

York Light Infantry Volunteers See MAA 294 *British Forces in the West Indies 1793-1815*.

York Rangers Authorised raised from 22.7.1803 by LtCol Stevenson, this unit was to recruit blacks for eventual service in the colonies. In March 1804 there were 87 blacks, most from the French West Indies, with 40 East Indians. The unit was based on the Isle of Wight. Recruiting was slow, and on 24.3.1805 the regiment was disbanded. There were then about 200 men recruited, and these were sent to the Royal African Corps (qv) with their arms, accoutrements and uniforms. The European sergeants and drummers were transferred to British line regiments. *Uniform:* As the 5th Rifle Bn, 60th Foot.

Baron Louis de Roll was a former captain in the Swiss Guards in French service who barely escaped the massacre at the Tuileries palace on 10 August 1792. He devoted the rest of his life to fighting Republican and Imperial France; two years later he raised his own Swiss regiment, which proved to be one of the best and longest serving foreign units in the British forces. The baron was an ardent freemason, as can be seen by the insignia he chose for his corps.

SELECT BIBLIOGRAPHY

Archive documents consulted are in the Public Records Office, Colonial Office (cited as PRO, CO) and War Office (PRO, WO); also at the National Archives of Canada (NAC). Manuscripts by Charles Hamilton Smith are at the Houghton Library, Harvard University (C.H. Smith MS). Herbert's lace books are at the National Army Museum, London, and Pearse's tailoring notes at the Canadian War Museum. Notebooks of the Rev.Percy Sumner are at the Anne S.K.Brown Military Collection, Brown University, Rhode Island.

Atkinson, C.T., 'The British capture of Genoa, 1814', *Journal of the Royal United Service Institution*, LX, November 1915

Atkinson, C.T., 'The Foreign Elements in the British Army 1793-1815', *Journal of the Royal United Service Institution*, LVIII, March 1914

Boppe, P., *La Croatie militaire*, Paris, 1900

Bovay, E.H., *Le Canada et les Suisses 1604-1974*, Fribourg, 1976

Brett-James, Anthony, ed., *Edward Costello: Military Memoirs, Adventures of a Soldier*, London 1967

Butler, Lewis & Hare, Sir Stewart, *The Annals of the King's Royal Rifle Corps*, London 1913, Vols. 3 & 4 and separate volume appendix on uniform, armament and equipment by S.M.Milnes & Astley Terry with plates by P.W.Reynolds

Connolly, T.W.J., *The History of the Corps of Sappers and Miners*, London 1855, Vol.1

Crooks, J.J., *Historical Records of the Royal African Corps*, Dublin, 1925

Dempsey, Guy C., 'Mutiny at Malta', *Journal of the Society for Army Historical Research*, LXVII, 1989

Fortescue, John W., *A History of the British Army*, London 1912-1923, Vols. VII-XI

Gould, Robert W., *Mercenaries of the Napoleonic Wars*, Brighton 1995

Grouvel, Vicomte de, *Les troupes de l'Émigration française*, Paris 1957, Vol. 1

Harfield, Alan, *British & Indian Armies in the East Indies 1685-1935*, Chippenham 1984

Hayter, Alethea, ed., *The Backbone: Diaries of a Military Family in the Napoleonic Wars*, Durham 1993

Lawson, Cecil C.P., *A History of the Uniforms of the British Army*, Vol.V, London 1967

Puccemulton, Domenico, 'Giornale della guerra combattuta nella parte orientale della Spagna dall' esxercito Anglo-Napolitano comandato da Lord Bentink', *Ancologia Militare*, c. 1834

Smith, Charles Hamilton, *Costume of the Army of the British Empire*, London 1815

Statement respecting the Earl of Selkirk's settlement upon the Red River... , London 1817

Tylden, G., *The Armed Forces of South Africa*, Johannesburg 1954

Louis de Watteville (1776-1836) served in Flanders in 1793-95, and in Switzerland in 1799-1800. Lieutenant-colonel of De Watteville's Regiment in 1801, he was present in Egypt in 1801 and at Maida in 1806. He became colonel of the regiment in 1812, a major-general in 1813, and was in Canada in 1813-16. (Print after portrait)

THE PLATES

A: SOUTHERN ITALY

A1: Private, Watteville's Swiss Regiment, 1803

Colonel de Watteville noted that 'the regiment's dress for that year [1803] was a red coat, green collar and facings'. The term facings applied to lapels and cuffs for officers and cuffs only for enlisted men. The green facings did not last long, as the regiment obviously wished to have its traditional black facings. (Col de Watteville's diary, copy at NAC)

A2: Private, Chasseurs Britanniques, c.1806-1809

The men's uniform was a red coatee with sky blue collar and cuffs, white turnbacks, and pointed white lace with a red and a sky blue line in even spacing. The unit had the distinctions of light infantry regiments in the British service and also had black accoutrements.

A3: Bugler, Royal Corsican Rangers, c.1808

The clothier Pearse noted for the 'Bugle jacket, 36 yards of cord, 44 buttons, scarlet facings'. A sample of the bugler's jacket cord was pasted on the page; it was made with two dark green strands and one red strand twisted together. The regimental uniform was to be the same as that of the 5th Bn, 60th Foot. Pearse also mentions 'Corsican, Private jacket, bottle green, 44 breast [pewter] buttons, red collar, cuffs and [shoulder] straps, 3 yards of red binding for feathering [piping]. Sergeants scarlet facings.' The pantaloons were green, the accoutrements black, and the black cylindrical shako had a white metal bugle horn badge and a green plume. The regimental uniform may have changed from 1813, as Hamilton Smith's chart indicates a red jacket with red collar and cuffs, three rows of pewter buttons on the chest, and dark sky blue pantaloons.

B: AFRICA

B1: Private, Cape Regiment, 1806-1808

The 'Hottentot' or 'Cape Native Regiment' initially had grey jackets, apparently plain, with white linen trousers, black shakos with a green tuft and probably a bugle badge, sandals, and canvas bayonet and pouch belts. It was later issued with black infantry accoutrements. (PRO, CO 48/3 and, WO 1/635)

B2: Drummer, Royal African Corps, c.1810

The drummer's red coatee had blue cuffs, collar, shoulder straps and wings, trimmed with regimental lace at the buttonholes and broad lace at the seams and edging the cuffs; the drummer's broad lace was $^5/_8$in wide with a yellow and black centre, each side white with a red line. (Pearse)

B3: Officer, Royal African Corps, 1808

The officers of the corps were allowed a simplified practical uniform in 1808. It consisted of a scarlet single-breasted coatee with blue collar and cuffs, short white turnbacks like the men's coatees, gilt buttons set equidistant with twist cord trim at the buttonholes (blue on collar and cuffs, scarlet elsewhere), and gold lace shoulder straps rather than epaulettes. This was worn with a black round hat with plume and cockade; white cotton or India dimity waistcoat; white trousers of the same material, to be worn loose and tied

LtCol Charles MacCarthy (1764-1823), Royal African Corps, 1812. This officer had a colourful career in Britain's small and pestilential West African colonies, which would eventually be the death of him. He was born in Cork in 1764 of French and Irish parents, and entered French service as a junior officer in Berwick's Irish Regiment in 1785. Joining the Royalist émigrés in 1791, he was appointed lieutenant-colonel of the Royal African Corps and governor of Senegal and Goree until 1814, and thereafter governor of Sierra Leone. His small forces suffered a disastrous defeat at the hands of the Ashantis in 1823, in which he perished. Officers had gold buttons and epaulettes but no lace on their regulation uniform. Epaulettes were replaced by wings from 1817 (Herbert's). A memorandum of 1808, however, reveals a more practical dress to be worn by the officers of the corps - see Plate B. (National Army Museum, London, 10140)

round the ankle with tape; half-gaiters of white cotton or dimity, shoes and black leather stock. On duty the crimson sash and gorget were added, with the regulation sword worn on a black shoulder belt; the off-duty sidearm was a dirk suspended from a black waistbelt with round gilt lion's-mask clasps. (Sumner, P., 'Cox & Co. Army Agents', *Journal of the Society for Army Historical Research*, XVII, 1938)

C: MALTA

C1: Sergeant, Maltese Military Artificers, 1808-1815

The two companies in Malta had, from 1806, a blue jacket with black collar and cuffs, brass Ordnance buttons, blue cloth pantaloons, and probably a round hat with feather. From 1808 white cotton uniforms made on the island with black collar and cuffs were issued instead, as they were less expensive and better adapted to the climate. Weapons were

Calabrian Free Corps, fusiliers and officer, c.1813-1814. This French print shows what may have been the last uniform of the corps when serving in south-east Spain - blue, including the pantaloons, with yellow facings at collar and cuffs. See also Plate D. (Print after Martinet)

OPPOSITE **Riflemen of the 2nd Regiment, Greek Light Infantry, 1814. Red skull cap with brass plate and green tuft; red short jacket with green cuffs and broad green tape piped with yellow, no buttons; red waistcoat with green tape piped with yellow and brass buttons; white *fustanella* (Greek kilt) and breeches; red stockings, buff Greek shoes; black rifle accoutrements, and small powder horn on green cord fixed to shoulder belt; armed with pistol, rifle and sword bayonet. (Print after C.H.Smith; Anne S.K.Brown Military Collection, Brown University, Providence; photo R.Chartrand)**

not carried. Sergeants were distinguished by a sash and corporals by chevrons only; the sergeant-major wore the same uniform as his British counterpart. The Maltese adjutant had the same dress as officers of the Royal Engineers. See illustrations for the dress of the 'war company' in Gibraltar.

C2: Officer, 1st Malta Provincial Battalion, 1802-1806

The battalions had red coatees, collar and cuffs in the facing colour, white turnbacks, white buttonhole lace and pewter buttons; white breeches and black gaiters; black round hats with white-over-red tufts were later replaced by shakos. The men also had white linen or cotton jackets and pantaloons, short black gaiters, leather fatigue caps and knapsacks. The 1st Bn had sky blue facings with silver buttons and lace for the officers; the 2nd Bn had green facings with gold buttons and lace. Accoutrements were black until changed to white in 1812. A period caricature shows the colonel wearing a round hat with a white-over-red plume. (Marrion, Robert J. 'Regiments of Malta', *Military Modelling*, April & May 1990)

C3: Drummer, Royal Regiment of Malta, 1805-1811

The regimental drummers wore a red coatee with blue collar, cuffs and wings, white turnbacks, white broad lace with small blue chevrons at the centre square-ended and set evenly and pewter buttons; white breeches, black gaiters, and a black stovepipe shako with a brass plate completed the uniform. (Pearse)

D: THE EASTERN MEDITERRANEAN
D1: Field officer, 2nd Greek Light Infantry, 1814

This figure, based on a Denis Dighton painting in the Royal Collection, may possibly be Sir Richard Church himself. It shows the 'Greek' uniform with the added neo-classical influences of the nascent Romantic period. Note in particular he helmet, the greaves for the lower legs, and the gilt knee-protectors bearing lion's heads. The crimson velvet jacket is richly embroidered with gold and has green cuffs, the facing colour of the 2nd Greek Light Infantry. This dress was probably worn by those British officers who became especially fond of Greece, such as Church. After the Napoleonic Wars Church went back to Greece to fight the Ottoman Turks for the country's independence. Lord Byron, the celebrated poet, joined him; Byron died of fever, but Church became a leading general of the Greek army. When he retired in 1843 he was hailed as a key figure in the struggle for Greek liberation. (PRO, WO 26/42; Fosten, Don, 'Greek Light Infantry', *Military Modelling*, December 1992)

D2: Fusilier, Sicilian Regiment, c.1810

According to a c.1810 entry in the Pearse notebook, the enlisted men had a red 'private jacket, 10 by 2 double headed, 12 yards looping lace, 30 small buttons, dark green facings'; a piece of white lace with a green central line is pasted on the page. For the 'drum [actually bugler's] coat, 30 small buttons, broad lace seams frames, body and cuffs, 10 yards broad lace, 15 yards of narrow'. The buglers would have had a green coatee with red collar and cuffs with the lace edging the seams but without sleeve chevrons. The officers had gold buttons; their wings of dark green had plain gold scales and 'flat braid on each side', with silver bugle and 'no bullions' fringes. Gold bugle with laurel badges on dark green decorated the turnbacks; and there was a gold lace triangle at the rear waist (Herbert's). The chaplain was to wear a black cassock with the crucifix hanging from his neck and a tassel on his priest's cap. The 1813 standing orders mention a 'casco' for head dress, which has been interpreted as a helmet - but 'casco' could also mean cap, which was synonymous with shako; we have opted for the latter as the more typical and less expensive headgear. (Pearse Notebook, Canadian War Museum; Fosten, Don, 'His Majesty's Sicilian Regiment', *Military Modelling*, November 1990)

D3: Fusilier, Calabrian Free Corps, 1809-1811

The first uniform of the corps was probably made in Sicily and is shown in an Italian print of the period, upon which this reconstruction is based. It featured a blue open jacket, faced yellow, with many buttons and narrow braid; a blue waistcoat, a pair of blue trousers, and a high-crowned conical round hat with a wide brim turned up on the left side. This was the dress of the regiment when it participated at the capture of Santa Maura in the Ionian Islands in April 1810. (Dempsey, Guy C., 'The Calabrian Free Corps in British Service 1809-1814', *Journal of the Society for Army Historical Research*, LXII, 1984)

E: PORTUGAL & SPAIN

E1: Field officer, Chasseurs Britanniques, c.1810-1814

The officers had silver buttons, lace and epaulettes. The facings in this unit were usually edged with lace rather than following the usual practice of lacing the buttonholes. Our subject is shown in typical campaign dress with overalls and a cover for his bicorn hat. The c.1813 full dress coatee had 18 yards of silver lace, silver epaulettes with scale straps and gilt bugle badges, and turnbacks with silver bugles. (Herbert's)

E2: Sergeant, Dillon's Regiment, 1813-1814

The enlisted men had red coatees with yellow collar and cuffs, white turnbacks, white bastion-shaped lace with a black line set evenly, and pewter buttons. In October 1811 the regiment was sent '1,400 suits of slop clothing, con-

sisting of cloth caps, jackets and trousers' with greatcoats, shirts, half-stockings and shoes. Sergeants had the usual distinctions: plain white lace, three chevrons on the right sleeve, crimson sash with yellow line, sword and pike. Officers had silver buttons and lace and turnback decorations of silver crow's-feet on yellow. (PRO, WO 6/173).

E3: Drummer, Roll's Swiss Regiment, 1813-1814

Drummers wore the traditional reversed colours - dark sky blue coatee with red collar, cuffs and wings; their white lace with a red stripe decorated the buttonholes and all seams and appeared as three double chevrons, points down, on each sleeve. The dark sky blue drum had a white sphinx within laurels, and red hoops. The drum-major had red lapels, silver lace, and a bicorn laced silver edged with red plumes and a standing white-over-red plume.

F: MAURITIUS & CEYLON

F1: Private, Rifle Company, 2nd Ceylon Regiment, c.1803

The 2nd's rifle company had dark green coatees with scarlet collar and cuffs, its officers black cords with gold buttons and wings. The 2nd Regiment wore this blue headgear in place of shakos as it was recruited from Indian sepoys.

F2: Fusilier, Bourbon Regiment, 1810-1812

Initially, the regiment had no regular uniform but was 'very neatly and uniformly clothed in nankeen', which appears to have consisted of a round jacket and pantaloons of a yellowish colour, most likely with a round hat. This temporary uniform was provided at the request of the men against deductions from their pay. The arms were in good order and all English; the belts were also good, but the cartridge boxes were deemed very bad by April 1812. Mounted officers had blue housings but their dress is not recorded (PRO, WO 27/108, pt 1). In London, on 15 April 1812, the Prince Regent approved that the regiment should be 'clothed and equipped in a like manner as the 95th or Rifle Corps' (PRO, WO 3/203). This uniform was sent to Mauritius and issued on Christmas Day 1813. Only the light company had rifles, the rest of the regiment being armed with muskets. Accoutrements were described in 1815 as being 'black waistbelts', which seem to indicate that rifle accoutrements were issued to everyone (PRO, WO 27/108, 113 and 135)

F3: Private, 1st Ceylon Regiment, c.1803-1814

The Malay-recruited 1st Regiment had a red coatee with buff collar, cuffs and turnbacks, white lace square-ended and singly spaced, pewter buttons, white pantaloons, no shoes and a 'stovepipe' shako. Besides the issue muskets and bayonets Malays also carried their wavy-bladed *kris* daggers. The officers had gold buttons, gold vellum lace, and gold double crow's-foot turnback ornaments on scarlet; however, no lace was to be worn on the coatee after 1813 except for half crow's-feet on the turnbacks. The rifle company was dressed in green, possibly like the rifle companies of the 60th. (G.L.W.Watson, 'The First Malay Regiment 1796-1874' *Malaya in History*, July 1957; Herbert's lace book)

G: CANADA

G1: Officer with colours, Meuron's Swiss Regiment, 1813-1816

Officers had silver buttons, lace and epaulettes, and turnback ornaments of a silver crow's-foot on yellow filled scarlet. The colours were of the traditional Swiss design having a yellow cross bearing the motto in gold letters, and the quarters filled with wavy flames of the colonel's livery colour (green, black and yellow) - except for the first canton which bore the British Union flag. (Meuron, Guy de, *Le Régiment Meuron 1781-1816*, Lausanne 1982)

The Bourbon Regiment raised in Mauritius and La Réunion had a similar uniform to this private of the 95th Rifles in 1815, but the men were blacks or mulattoes from the islands. Most were armed with smooth-bore muskets, only the élite rifle company being armed and equipped as shown. See Plate F. (Print after Genty)

G2: Fusilier, Meuron's Swiss Regiment, 1813-1816

The men wore a red coatee with sky blue collar and cuffs, white bastion-shaped lace with a red line, white turnbacks and pewter buttons, initially with white breeches and the stovepipe shako. Grey pantaloons, short grey gaiters and the 'Belgic' shako were taken into wear from 1812. Drummers were said to have been dressed 'in the colours of the Colonel which are green black and yellow'. Their coatees had 8½ yards of broad lace at the seams and cuffs, and 15 yards of narrow lace. The broad lace was 1⅛ inch wide and quite complicated, with black and yellow central bars with white edges having green and red lines. The men with Lord Selkirk in 1816-17 'retained their [military] clothing'.

G3: Officer, Light Company, Watteville's Swiss Regiment, 1813-1816

Colonel de Watteville reported that 'the regiment's dress for that year [1804] was a red coat, black collar and facings'. This remained the regimental uniform until its disbandment. The men's lace was white with a black line, set on in bastion shape; the coatee had pewter buttons and white turnbacks. The 1812 clothing did not reach the regiment, so it landed in Canada with its 1811 issue. The 1813 clothing, which included grey pantaloons, arrived in Canada in June and was issued to the men in Montreal before they left for Kingston. The 1814 issue was received in May of that year. Officers had silver buttons and square-ended lace set in pairs, and their black velvet facings were piped with white. In 1813 the officer's dress coatee had silver epaulettes with 'round top, corded, edged with black velvet, crescent round cord & filled bullion'. The turnbacks had a silver crow's-foot on black velvet (Herbert). Some 1807-13 clothing bills reveal that the officers of the grenadier company had fur caps with 'Rich gold cord, band silver, Embroidered grenade, silver Sphinx, gilt plate & white feather'; that all officers had white pantaloons in 1810 and grey in 1812; and that the chaplain had black pantaloons. The regiment had special badges; from January 1805 'A Sphynx and a crown of laurels with the word EGYPT' were embroidered on the colours, and in 1807 the honour 'Maida'. Surviving badges and buttons bear these distinctions. (NAC, MG54, N23)

H: ITALIAN UNITS

H1: Carabinier, Italian Levy, 1812-1815

In his uniform manuscript now at Harvard University, Hamilton Smith shows a small figure in the regiment's uniform with the collar edged all around with white lace, buttons at the top of the cuffs, green tufts at the possibly green shoulder straps, a cylindrical black shako with an indistinct small brass badge possibly meant to be a bugle horn and a green plume, and white accoutrements with a brass belt plate. The green items most likely indicate a light infantry carabinier, who would be armed with a British musket and bayonet.

H2: Captain, Italian Levy, 1812-1815

Officers had 'a blue jacket with skirts, single breasted with red cuffs and collar, the skirts turned back with white, the lining and edges of the jacket red, yellow buttons, the lieutenant colonel to be distinguished by two rows of lace round the cuffs, the majors by one. The buttons of the

Charles-Philippe de Bosset (1773-1845), lieutenant-colonel of Roll's Swiss Regiment, c.1812. Officers of Roll's wore scarlet faced with a dark sky blue and trimmed with silver lace and buttons, but no skirt ornaments. The regimental lace was supposed to be in pointed loops with a small false tassel, but there is no sign of this feature in this portrait. The edges of the collar, cuffs and lapels were piped with white. For undress occasions officers wore a small dirk from a narrow black waist belt; and a round hat with a flat braid band was reported in 1813 (Herbert's). (Print after portrait)

captains to be put on by two and two, those of the subalterns at equal distances. Grey cloth pantaloons and half boots or gaiters. The officers are to wear caps [shakos] similar to those of the men with four inch feathers, red silk sashes, and crimson and gold sword knots are to be worn. Officers to wear black waistbelts.' (PRO, WO 1/311)

H3: Fusilier, Piedmontese Legion, 1814

The legion's uniform was a blue coatee with red cuffs and turnbacks (and probably collar too), brass buttons, blue pantaloons, short gaiters, shoes, black cravat or stock with clasp, shirt, stockings, and a felt shako possibly of the 'Belgic' type. Articles shipped with the legion in June 1814 included blue jackets and trousers, black gaiters, shakos and plumes, blue cloth undress caps, undress white jackets and trousers, stocks, stockings, greatcoats, canteens and knapsacks. (Schiavo, Vittorio, 'Notizie intorno alla formazione di una legione piemontese in Inghilterra in età napoleonica', *Studi Piemontesi*, Nov. 1989, XVIII, No.2; PRO, WO 1/659)

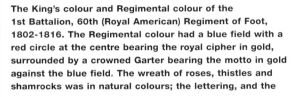

The King's colour and Regimental colour of the
1st Battalion, 60th (Royal American) Regiment of Foot,
1802-1816. The Regimental colour had a blue field with a
red circle at the centre bearing the royal cipher in gold,
surrounded by a crowned Garter bearing the motto in gold
against the blue field. The wreath of roses, thistles and
shamrocks was in natural colours; the lettering, and the
crowned ciphers in three corners, were in gold. The
1st Battalion spent the period up to 1810 in Jamaica, and
thereafter served at the Cape of Good Hope - whose healthy
climate must have seemed like paradise after the fever-
ridden West Indies. In 1815 an inspection reported only nine
British soldiers in the ranks of this predominantly German
and Swiss unit.

COMPANION SERIES FROM OSPREY

CAMPAIGN

Concise, authoritative accounts of history's decisive military
encounters. Each 96-page book contains over 90 illustrations
including maps, orders of battle, colour plates, and
three-dimensional battle maps.

WARRIOR

Definitive analysis of the appearance, weapons, equipment,
tactics, character and conditions of service of the individual
fighting man throughout history. Each 64-page book includes
full-colour uniform studies in close detail, and sectional
artwork of the soldier's equipment.

NEW VANGUARD

Comprehensive histories of the design, development and
operational use of the world's armoured vehicles and artillery.
Each 48-page book contains eight pages of full-colour
artwork including a detailed cutaway.

ORDER OF BATTLE

The most detailed information ever published on the units
which fought history's great battles. Each 96-page book
contains comprehensive organisation diagrams supported by
ultra-detailed colour maps. Each title also includes a large
fold-out base map.

ELITE

Detailed information on the organisation, appearance
and fighting record of the world's most famous military
bodies. This series of 64-page books, each containing
some 50 photographs and diagrams and 12 full-colour
plates, will broaden in scope to cover personalities,
significant military techniques, and other aspects of
the history of warfare which demand a comprehensive
illustrated treatment.

AIRCRAFT OF THE ACES

Focuses exclusively on the elite pilots of major air
campaigns, and includes unique interviews with surviving
aces sourced specifically for each volume. Each 96-page
volume contains up to 40 specially commissioned artworks,
unit listings, new scale plans and the best archival
photography available.

COMBAT AIRCRAFT

Technical information from the world's leading aviation
writers on the century's most significant military aircraft.
Each 96-page volume contains up to 40 specially
commissioned artworks, unit listings, new scale plans
and the best archival photography available.

COPYRIGHT

Eleven Horror Short Stories by Horacio Quiroga. Translation and compilation by Joaquin de la Sierra.

ACKNOWLEDG-MENTS

I would not have been able to translate this book without the help of 12 supporters who believed in my project and decided to back it on Kickstarter. Thank you so much. Here are their names:

Dylan Mooney, Mary Gaitan, Joseph Cox, Visakh, Brandy Pastore, Adi Gurovich, Johann Strauss, Robert Smith, Yontalcar, William Patrick Davis, and Megan Thomas.

Special thanks to Paul Leone, the main sponsor of this book.

There are countless books written in Spanish that have not been translated into English and are now largely forgotten. My mission is to make some of these works more widely available. Please sign up on this page If you wish me to notify you when I launch a new project. I am eternally thankful to everyone who supports my projects.

CONTENTS

THE SPECTRE

Every night at the Grand Splendid in Santa Fe, Enid and I go to movie premieres. Neither storms nor frosty nights have prevented us from entering, at ten o'clock, into the warm gloom of the theater.

From one balcony or another, it doesn't matter; because the location is indifferent to us. And even if the theater is sold out some night, because the movie *The Splendid* is in full swing, we settle down, mute, always attentive to the film in any already occupied balcony. We don't interrupt anyone, I think, at least noticeably.

Enid and I, apart from the world around us, are all eyes towards the screen from the balcony's back.

And if someone, feeling chills with an unexplainable origin, sometimes turns around to investigate or feels an icy breath coming from nowhere, our presence of intruders goes unnoticed, for it is necessary to warn now that Enid and I are dead.

Of all the women I met in the living world,

none affected me as Enid. Her impression was so strong; it erased the memory of any other beautiful woman who I ever met. In my soul, dark as night, a single imperishable star rose: Enid. The mere possibility of her eyes gazing at me without indifference made my heart abruptly stop. And at the thought that she could ever be mine, my jaw twitched. Enid!

When we were alive, she had the most divine beauty that the movie industry had launched and exposed to the fixed gaze of men. Above all, her eyes were unique; never did a velvet have a frame of lashes like Enid's eyes; blue, damp, and calm, like the happiness that sobbed in her.

Misfortune put me before her when she was already married. I will not hide any names. Everyone remembers Duncan Wyoming, the extraordinary actor. He, beginning his career at the same time as William Hart, had the same profound virtues of virile acting. Hart has given the movies everything we could hope for from him, and he is a falling star. On the other hand, of Wyoming, we don't know what we might have seen, when just at the beginning of his short and fantastic career, he created—in contrast to the sentimental hero of today—the rude, rough, ugly, kind of man.

Hart kept acting, and we have already watched him repeatedly. According to the official report, Wyoming was snatched from us in his prime age, at a time when two extraordinary tapes were ending: *El Paramo* and *Beyond What You See*.

But the charm—the absorption of all the feelings of a man—that Enid wielded on me had but one bitterness: Wyoming, who was her husband, was also my best friend.

I had not seen Duncan for two years; he was busy working, and I was busy studying. When I saw him again in Hollywood, he was already married.

"I introduce you to my wife," he said, throwing her into my arms.

He said to her: "Hold him tight, like a brother, because you won't have a friend like Grant. And kiss him if you want."

She did not kiss me, but when her hair caressed my neck, I felt a chill through all my nerves, making it clear that I could never be like a brother to that woman.

We lived in Canada for two months together, and it is not difficult to understand my state of mind regarding Enid. But not in a word, not in a movement, not in a gesture did I reveal my intentions to Wyoming. Only she read in my gaze, no matter how calm, how deeply I wanted her.

Love and desire were twins in me, sharp and mixed because if I desired her with all the might of my disembodied soul, I adored her with all the torrent of my substantial blood.

Duncan didn't notice. How could he?

We returned to Hollywood at the beginning of winter, and Wyoming then fell sick with the flu, which eventually cost him his life. He left his widow wealthy and childless. But he was not at peace because of the loneliness of his wife.

"It's not the economic situation," he told me, "but moral distress. And in this hell of the movie industry, it is worse."

On his death bed, lowering his wife and me to the pillow, and with pain in his voice, he said:

"Trust Grant, Enid ... As long as you have him, fear nothing. And you, old friend, watch over her. Be her brother. Now I can go to the other side in peace."

For some time, nothing changed in the pain Enid and I experienced. Seven days later, we returned to Canada to the same summer hut that had seen the three of us dine in front of the fireplace a month earlier. As then, Enid now gazed at the fire while I stood contemplating her. And Duncan was not with us anymore.

I must say it: in the death of Wyoming, I saw nothing but the liberation of the terrible eagle caged in the hearts of men, which is the desire of a woman that one cannot touch. I had been Wyoming's best friend, and while he lived, the eagle did not want her blood; He fed—I fed it—on my own. His wife was, while he lived—and would have been forever—intangible to me. But he had died. Wyoming could not demand the sacrifice of life in which he had just failed. And Enid was my life, my future, my encouragement, and my desire to live, which no one, not Duncan—my close friend, now dead—could deny me.

"Watch over her..." Those words resounded in my mind. Yes, I'll watch over her by giving her something important: the worship of a whole life devoted to her!

For two months, by her side day and night, I watched over her like a brother. But on the third, I fell at her feet.

Enid stared at me immobile, and surely the thought of Wyoming rose to her memory because she rejected me violently. But I did not remove my head from her skirt.

"I love you, Enid," I told her. "Without you, I prefer to die."

"You, Guillermo!" She murmured. "It is horrible to hear you say this!"

"Anything you want," I replied. "But I love you immensely."

"Shut up, shut up!"

"And I have always loved you … You know …"

"No, no, I do not know!"

"Yes, you know."

Enid always pushed me aside, and I resisted with my head between her knees.

"Tell me you knew …"

"No, shut up! We are desecrating the memory of Wyoming …"

"Tell me you knew …"

"Guillermo!"

"Just tell me that you knew that I have always loved you …"

Her arms gave up wearily, and I raised my head. I met her eyes instantly before Enid yielded to cry on her knees.

I left her alone, and when an hour later I came back in, white with snow, no one would have suspected, seeing our simulated and calm affection of every day, that we had just stretched, until we made them bleed, the strings of our hearts.

Because in the alliance of Enid and Wyoming, there had never been love. There was always a blaze of folly, misguidance, injustice—the flame of passion that burns a man's entire morale and burns a woman in long sobs of fire. Enid had loved her husband, nothing more, and she had wanted him, nothing more.

Death, then, left a gap that I had to fill with the affection of a brother. As a brother to her, Enid, was my only source of happiness in the entire world.

Three days after the scene I just related, we returned to Hollywood. And a month later, precisely the same situation was repeating itself: me again at Enid's feet with my head on her knees, as she kept pushing me away.

"I love you more every day, Enid ..."

"Guillermo!"

"Tell me that one day you will love me."

"No!"

"Just tell me that you know how much I love you."

"No!"

"Say it!"

"Leave me alone! Can't you see that you are making me suffer horribly?"

And when she felt me trembling mutely on her knees, she abruptly raised my face between her hands:

"But let me tell you! Let me! Don't you see that I also love you with all my soul and that we are committing a crime?"

Just four months, one hundred and twenty days barely elapsed since the death of the man she loved, of the friend who had interposed me like a protective veil between his wife and new love.

So deep and penetrating was our love that even today, I wonder with astonishment what absurd purpose our lives could have had if they had not found us under the arms of Wyoming.

One night—we were in New York—I found out that *El Páramo* was finally showing—one of the two films I have talked about and which release we eagerly awaited. I also had the keenest interest in seeing Enid, so I asked her to accompany me.

We looked at each other for a long time, an eternity of silence, during which the memory galloped backward between falling snow and dying faces. But Enid's gaze was life itself; between the damp velvet of her eyes and mine, she controlled the convulsive bliss of adoring each other and nothing more.

We went to the cinema, and from the reddish gloom of the balcony, we saw Duncan Wyoming appear, huge and with a face whiter than when he died. I felt Enid's arm tremble under my hand.

"Duncan!"

The same usual confident smile was on his lips. It was his energetic figure gliding along with the screen. And twenty meters from him was his own woman, who was holding hands with his close friend.

While the room was dark, neither Enid nor I spoke a word or stopped looking at each other for a moment. Long tears were rolling down her cheeks, and she was smiling at me. I was smiling without trying to hide her tears from me.

"Yes, I understand, my love," I murmured. "I understand, but let us not give up. Yes? We will forget."

Enid, always smiling at me, gathered herself mutely to my neck.

The next night we returned. Should we forget? The actor's presence, vibrant in the beam of light, transported him to the pulsating screen of life, his unconsciousness of the situation, his trust in the woman and his friend; we had to get used to all of this.

Over and over again, always attentive to the characters, we witnessed the growing success of *El Páramo*.

Wyoming's performance was outstanding, unfolding in a brute-energy drama: a small part in Canada's forests and the rest in New York itself. The central scene occurred when Wyoming, wounded in a fight with a man, abruptly had the revelation of his wife's love for this man, whom he had just killed for reasons other than their love. Wyoming had just tied a scarf to his forehead, and lying on the couch, still panting with fatigue, he witnessed the despair of his wife over the corpse of her lover.

Seldom has the revelation of collapse, desolation, and hatred come to the human face with more violent clarity than in Wyoming's eyes. The film's direction had squeezed that prodigy of expression to torture, and the scene was sustained for an infinite number of seconds when only one second was enough to show the red-white crisis of a heart in that state.

Enid and I, together and motionless in the dark, admired like nobody else the dead friend, whose eyelashes almost touched us when Wyoming came from the bottom to fill the screen. And as he walked away back to the scene of the set, the entire room seemed to respond accordingly. And Enid and I, slightly dizzy, felt the rub of Duncan's hair that had come to touch us.

Why did we keep going to the cinema? What deviation of our consciences led us there night after night to soak our pure love in blood? What omen was dragging us like sleepwalkers to the theater?

Where were his eyes looking? I don't know where—maybe to another balcony on our left. But one night, I noticed, I felt it in the roots of my hair, that the eyes were turning towards us. Enid must have seen it, too, because I felt the deep shake of her shoulders under my hand.

Natural laws and physical principles teach us about the photographic specters dancing on the screen, mimicking a lost life even in the most intimate details. It would be easier for us to see by our side a dead man who leaves the grave to accompany us than to perceive the slightest change of a livid face in a film.

Despite the laws and principles, Wyoming was watching us. *El Páramo* was a fictional movie, and Wyoming lived only by an irony of light. It was nothing more than an electric foil front without sides or bottom. For us—Wyoming, Enid, and I— the filmed scene lived flagrantly, not on the screen, but in a balcony.

Was Duncan's visible anger only the pretended hatred on that scene of *El Paramo*?

Of course not! There was the brutal revelation; the tender wife and the close friend in the showroom, laughing, heads together, at the trust placed in them.

But we quickly stopped laughing because night

by night, movie after movie, the gaze was turning more and more towards us.

"His gaze is coming closer and closer!" I said to myself.

"Tomorrow, he'll look straight at us." Enid thought.

As the cinema burned with light, the real world of physical laws took hold of us, and we breathed deeply.

But in the abrupt cessation of light, which we felt painfully on our nerves like a blow, the spectral drama caught us again.

A thousand leagues from New York, boxed under the ground, Duncan Wyoming lay buried without eyes. But his surprise at Enid's frenzied forgetfulness, his anger, and his revenge were alive there, igniting Wyoming's chemical trail, moving into his living eyes, which had finally just fixed on ours.

Enid gasped and hugged desperately to me.

"Guillermo!"

"Quiet, please."

"He has just taken one leg off the couch!"

I felt the skin on my back crawl, and I looked:

With extreme slowness and eyes fixed on us,

Wyoming rose from the couch. Enid and I saw him rise, advancing towards us from the back of the scene, coming to the foreground. A dazzling glare blinded us while Enid let out a cry.

The tape had just burned.

But in the lighted room, heads were all turned towards us. Some sat up to see what was happening.

"The lady is ill; she looks like a dead woman," said someone in the audience.

"He seems far worse," added another.

What else? Nothing, but the next day Enid and I did not see each other. Only, days after, when we first looked at each other at night to go to the cinema, Enid already had the darkness of the afterlife in her deep pupils, and I had a revolver in my pocket.

I do not know if anyone in the room recognized us as the sick couple from a few nights before. The lights went out, went on, and went out again, without my clenching fingers leaving the trigger for a moment.

The previous night, we didn't notice anything unusual on the screen, and Wyoming was still panting on the couch. But Enid—Enid in my arms —had her face turned to the light, ready to scream when Wyoming finally got up.

I saw him stand up, reach the very edge of the screen without taking his gaze from mine. I saw him come towards us in the beam of light; He came in the air over the heads of the audience, rising, coming up to us with his head bandaged. I saw him extend the claws of his fingers, just as Enid gave a horrible scream, the kind in which a vocal cord may rupture.

I can't tell what happened in the first instant. But after the first moments of confusion and smoke, I found myself with my body hanging off the balcony, dead.

From the moment Wyoming was sitting on the couch, I aimed the barrel of my revolver at his head. I remember it clearly. And it was I who had taken the bullet to the temple.

I am entirely sure I wanted to aim the gun at Duncan. Only, believing I was aiming at the murderer, I was aiming at myself. It was a mistake, a simple mistake, nothing more, but it cost me my life.

Three days later, Enid was, in turn, evicted from the world. And here our idyll ends.

But it is not over yet. A shot and a specter are not enough to vanish a love like ours. Beyond death, life, and their grudges, Enid and I have found each other. Invisible within the living world, Enid and I are always together, waiting for the announcement of another film premiere.

We have traveled the world. We have not seen *El Paramo* again. Wyoming's performance in it can no longer bring us surprises, as we have already paid dearly.

Now our hope is on *Beyond What Is Seen*. For seven years, the film company has announced its premiere, and Enid and I have waited. Duncan is its protagonist, but we will no longer be on the balcony, at least in our usual conditions. In the present circumstances, Duncan may make a mistake that allows us to re-enter the visible world in the same way that we, seven years ago, allowed him to animate the icy sheet of his film.

Enid and I now occupy, in the invisible fog of the disembodied, the privileged lurking spot that was Wyoming's entire force. If he persists, if he makes a mistake in seeing us and makes the slightest movement out of the grave, we will take advantage. The curtain separating life from death has not been drawn solely in favor of the living. Between the Nothingness that has dissolved what Wyoming was and the electric resurrection, there remains a space. With the most slight movement the actor makes, as soon as he detaches himself from the screen, Enid and I will slide as if through a fissure in the dark corridor. But we will not follow the road to Wyoming's grave; We will return to life, and it is the warm world, the tangible and vibrant love of every human sense, that awaits Enid and me then.

In a month or a year, the movie will arrive. We are only concerned about the possibility that *Beyond What Is Seen* will be released under another name, as is customary in this city. Therefore, we never miss a premiere. Night after night we enter the cinema at ten o'clock, where we settle in a balcony, either empty or already occupied, it does not matter.

THE BEYOND

"I was desperate," said the voice. "My parents were adamantly opposed to me having love affairs with him, and they had become very cruel to me. The last few days, they did not even let him show up at the door. Before, I saw him for just an instant standing on the corner, waiting for me since the morning. Afterward, not even that!"

I told my mother the week before:

"But what do you and Dad think of him? Why do you torture me like that? Do you have anything to say about him? Why have you objected, as if he were unworthy to set foot in this house, or even for him to visit me?"

Mom made me leave. Dad, who was coming in at that moment, stopped me by the arm, and when Mom found out what I had said, she pushed me out by the shoulder, throwing me from behind:

"Your mother is wrong; what she has meant is that she and I—do you hear it right?—we'd rather see you dead than in the arms of that man. And not a word more about this."

"Very well," I replied, turning, paler than the tablecloth itself, "I will never speak to you about him again."

And I entered my room slowly, deeply amazed to feel what I felt because, at that moment, I had decided to die.

Die! To finally let go of that everyday hell, knowing that he was two steps away, waiting to see me and suffering more than me! All because my father would never consent to my marriage with Luis. What didn't he approve? I still wonder. That he was poor? We were as much as he was.

Oh! I knew my father's stubbornness, as did my mother.

"Killed a thousand times," he said, "rather than giving her to that man."

But what did my father give me instead, if it wasn't the misfortune of loving with all my being knowing myself loved and condemned not even to see him at the door for a moment?

Dying was preferable, yes, dying together.

I knew that he could kill himself, but I, who alone did not find the strength to fulfill my destiny, felt that once at his side, I would prefer a thousand times death together to the despair of never seeing him again.

I wrote him a letter, willing to do anything. A week later, we were in the agreed place, and we were occupying a room in the same hotel.

I cannot say I was proud of what I was going to do, nor was I happy to die. It was something more fatal, more frantic, more without remission, as if from the depths of the past my grandparents, my great-grandparents, my childhood itself, my first communion, my dreams as if all this had no other purpose than to drive me to suicide.

We did not feel happy, I repeat, to die. We abandoned life because it had already left us by preventing us from being with each other. In the first, pure, and last hug that we gave each other on the bed, dressed and in shoes as when we arrived, I understood, marked with happiness in his arms, how great my joy would have been if I had become his girlfriend, his wife.

At once, we drank the poison. In the concise space of time between receiving the glass from his hand and bringing it to my mouth, those same forces of my parents that rushed me to death suddenly appeared on the edge of my destiny to stop me. Too late! Suddenly, all the noises from the street, from the city itself, ceased; they fell back vertiginously before me, leaving an enormous place in its hollow as if, up to that moment, a thousand familiar cries filled that area.

I remained still for two seconds, with my eyes open. And suddenly, I seized Luis convulsively, free at last from my dreadful loneliness.

Yes, I was with him; and we were going to die in an instant!

The poison was atrocious, and Luis first began the step that led us together to the grave.

"Forgive me," he said, still pressing my head against his neck. "I love you so much that I am taking you with me."

"And I love you," I replied, "and I die with you."

I could not speak anymore. But what sound of footsteps, what voices came from the corridor to indulge our agony? Who knocked on the door frantically?

"They followed me and came to separate us," I murmured still. "But I am all yours."

In the end, I realized that I had spoken those words in my mind because, at that moment, I was losing consciousness.

* * *

When I came to my senses, I thought I would fall if I did not look for a place to support myself. I felt light and so rested that even the sweetness of opening my eyes was sensitive to me. I was standing in the same hotel room, leaning almost against the far wall. And there, next to the bed, was my desperate mother.

So had they saved me? I turned my eyes to all sides, and next to the nightstand, standing like me, I saw Luis, who had just distinguished me in turn and came smiling. Despite the significant number of people around the bed, we went straight to each other, and we said nothing, for our eyes expressed all the happiness of being together.

Seeing him, diaphanous and visible through everything and everyone, I had just realized that I was like him: dead.

We had died; despite my fear of being saved when I lost consciousness, we had lost our lives, fortunately. And there, in bed, my desperate mother was screaming while the hotel waiter removed my arms from the head of my beloved.

Far in the background, with joined hands, Luis and I saw everything in a clear perspective, cold and without passion. Three steps away, without a doubt, we died by suicide, surrounded by the desolation of my relatives, the owner of the hotel, and the swaying of the police. What did we care about that?

"My love!" Luis said to me. "At what little price have we bought our eternal happiness!"

"And I," I replied, "will always love you as I loved

you before. And we will not part anymore, right?"

"Oh no! ... We've already tried it."

"And are you going to visit me every night?"

While we were exchanging our promises, we heard my mother's violent screams, which reached us with an inert sound and no echo as if they could not penetrate the environment that surrounded Mom by more than a meter.

We looked back inside the room. Two men were carrying our corpses at last, and it must have been a long time since we died, for we could see that both Luis and I already had rigid joints and very stiff fingers.

Our bodies lay there. Had there been something of our life, our tenderness, in those two weighty bodies that came down the stairs, threatening to roll everyone with them?

Dead! How absurd! What had lived in us, more potent than life itself, continued to live with all the hopes of eternal love. Before, I had not even been able to peek out the door to see him; now, I would regularly talk to him, and he would come home as my boyfriend.

"When are you going to visit me?" I asked.

"Tomorrow," he said. "Let us rest today."

"Why tomorrow?" I asked, frantic. "Isn't it the

same today? Come tonight, Luis! I want to be alone with you in the living room!"

"Me too! At nine, then?"

"Yes. See you later, my love..."

And we parted ways. I returned home slowly, happy and relieved, as if it were the first date of my life.

* * *

At nine o'clock I ran to the front door and received my boyfriend myself. He is home, visiting!

"Do you know that the room is full of people?"— I asked—"But they won't bother us."

"Of course not ... Is your corpse there?"

"Yes."

"Very disfigured?"

"Not much at all. Come, let's see!"

We entered the room. Despite the temples' lividness and the very tight nostrils, my face was almost the same as Luis expected to see.

"You look very similar," he said.

"Right?" I replied, happy. And we immediately forgot everything, lulling each other.

At times, however, we suspended our conversation and watched the crowd go in and out. In one of those moments, I caught Luis' attention.

"Look!"—I said—"What do you think will happen?"

Indeed, the entry into the room of a new coffin agitated everyone in the room. New people, not yet seen there, accompanied it.

"It's me," Luis said with slight surprise. "My sisters come too."

"Look, Luis!" I observed. "They put our corpses in the exact position as we were when we died."

"As we should always be," he added, fixing his eyes for a long time on the face excavated with the pain of his sisters:

"Poor girls ..." he murmured with grave tenderness. I got close to him, won by the belated homage but bloody atonement, overcoming who knows what difficulties my parents made by burying us together.

"They are burying us. What madness!" Lovers who have committed suicide on a hotel bed, pure in body and soul, live forever. Nothing linked us to those two cold and rigid bodies, now nameless. And despite everything, however, they had been too dear to us in another existence for us not to cast a long look full of memories on those two cadaverous ghosts of love.

"Our corpses too," said my beloved, "will be together forever."

"But I'm with you," I murmured, raising my eyes to him happily. And we forgot everything again.

* * *

For three months, I lived in total bliss. My boyfriend visited me twice a week. He would arrive at nine o'clock, without a second of delay. My boyfriend was not always so punctual to leave. Eleventhirty, even twelve, without him deciding to let go of my hands, without me being able to tear my gaze from his.

During the day, I shortened the hours by thinking about him. I went back and forth from room to room, watching my family's movement without any interest. However, more than once, I stopped at the dining room door to contemplate the gloomy pain of my mother, who sometimes broke into desperate sobs at the empty place of the table where her youngest daughter used to sit down.

I lived—survived—by love and for love. Outside of him, my loved one, and the presence of his memory, everything acted for me in a world apart. And even when I was close to my family, an invisible and transparent abyss opened between them and me, separating us a thousand leagues.

Luis and I also went out at night, as the official

couple that we were. There is no walk that we have not traveled together, nor twilight in which we have not slipped our idyll. When there was a full moon, and the temperature was cool at night, we liked to extend our walks to the city's outskirts, where we felt freer, purer, and more loving.

One of those nights, as our footsteps had brought us to the view of the cemetery, we were curious to see where our corpses were lying underground. We entered the vast enclosure and stopped before a dark patch of land, where a marble tombstone gleamed. It only bore our two names, and underneath the date of our death, nothing more.

"As I remember us," Luis observed, "it couldn't be shorter. Still," he added after a pause, "it contains more tears and regrets than many long epitaphs."

After he said that, we were silent again.

Perhaps in that place and at that hour, we would have given the impression of being foolish to those who observed us. But my boyfriend and I knew well that what was fatuous and without redemption were those two specters of a double suicide locked up at our feet, and reality, life purified of errors, rose pure and sublimated in us like two flames of the same love.

We left there, happy and without memories, to

walk along the white road, our happiness without limits.

Isolated from the world, with no other end or other thought than to see each other for the sake of seeing each other, our love ascended. We both began to feel a lovely melancholy when we were together and extreme sadness when we were apart. I forgot to say that my boyfriend visited me every night then, but we spent almost all the time without speaking as if our phrases of affection had no value to express what we felt. He retired later when everyone was asleep at home, and when he left, we shortened our farewell.

We went out and returned speechless because I knew well that what he could say to me did not respond to his thoughts, and he was sure that I would answer him anything, to avoid looking at him.

One night when our uneasiness had reached an unbearable limit, Luis said goodbye to me later than usual. And as he extended his hands to me, and I gave him my frozen ones, I read in his eyes, with intolerable transparency, what was happening to us. I turned as pale as death itself, and his hands did not let go of mine.

"Luis!" I murmured in horror, feeling that my disembodied life was desperately seeking support, as in any other circumstance. He understood our situation's horribleness because releasing my

27

hands with a courage that I now appreciate; his eyes regained unmistakable tenderness.

"See you tomorrow, my love," he said, smiling.

"See you tomorrow, love," I murmured, paling even more as I said this.

Because in that instant, I had just realized that I would never be able to utter these words again.

Luis returned the next night; we went out together, talked, and talked like we never had before. All in vain: we could no longer look at each other. We said goodbye briefly, without touching each other.

Last night my boyfriend fell suddenly before me and put his head on my knees.

"My love," he murmured.

"Shut up!"—I said.

"My love," he began.

"Luis! Shut up!" I replied, terrified. "If you repeat that..."

His head rose, and our ghostly eyes—this is horrible to say! —Met for the first time in many days.

"What?" Luis asked. "What if I say it?"

"You know what happens," I replied.

"Tell me!"

"You know! I'm dying!"

For fifteen seconds, we linked our gazes with tremendous fixation. In that time, running as if by the thread of destiny, endless love stories truncated, resumed, broken, revived, defeated, and finally sunk in the dread of the impossible.

"I'm dying ..." I began to murmur, responding to his gaze. He understood it, too, for sinking his forehead back into my knees, he raised his voice for a long time.

"We have but one thing to do ..." he said.

"I think so," I said.

"You understand me?" Luis insisted.

"Yes, I understand you," I replied, placing my hands on his head so that he would let me sit up. And without looking back, we headed to the cemetery.

One does not play at life, at sobbing passion, when from the bottom of a coffin two corpses ask us to account for our imitation and our falsehood! Love! An unpronounceable word when used after taking a cup of cyanide to die!

"That kiss cost us our lives," the voice concludes, "and we know it."

When you have died once of love, you must die

again. A while ago, when Luis picked up himself, I would have given up my soul to be kissed. In an instant, he will kiss me, and what in us was sublime and unsustainable fictional fog will descend, vanish at the critical and always faithful contact of our mortal remains.

I do not know what awaits us beyond. But if our love was one day capable of rising over our poisoned bodies and managed to live for three months in the hallucination of an idyll, perhaps a primitive and essential urn of that love has resisted the contingencies that await us.

Standing on the tombstone, Luis and I look at each other long and freely. His arms encircle my waist, his mouth seeks my mouth, and I give him a deep kiss with such passion that I vanish.

THE ARTIFICIAL HELL

On nights when the moon is visible, the gravedigger advances through the tombs with a singularly stiff step. He walks shirtless and wears a large straw hat. His smile, fixed, gives the sensation of being glued to the face. If he were barefoot, it would be noticeable that he walks with the toes bent down.

There is nothing strange about this because the gravedigger regularly ingests chloroform. A few incidents have led him to try the anesthetic, and when chloroform becomes part of a man's life, it rarely lets go. Our acquaintance waits for the night to open his bottle, and as he is a prudent man, he chooses the cemetery as the inviolable theater of his drunkenness.

Chloroform dilates the chest on the first breath; on the second, it floods the mouth with saliva; on the third, the limbs tingle; on the fourth, the lips, along with weird ideas, swell, and then unbelievable things happen.

Eventually, the fantasy of his death led the gravedigger to an open grave in which he removed most of the bones that afternoon—an unfinished affair for lack of time. A coffin lay open behind the gate, and next to it, the skeleton of the man locked inside.

Has he heard anything? Our acquaintance unlocks the bolt, enters, and after turning to see the man's skeleton, kneels and looks deeply at the skull's orbits.

There, at the bottom, a little higher than the base of the skull, is huddled a shivering little man, yellow, his face crossed with wrinkles. His mouth is purple, his eyes are deeply sunken, and he looks anxious.

"This is all that's left of a cocaine addict."

"Cocaine! Please, some cocaine!"

The serene gravedigger knows well that he would dissolve the glass in his flask with saliva to reach the prohibited chloroform. So it's his duty to help the shivering little man.

He leaves and returns with the entire syringe, which the cemetery medicine cabinet has provided for him.

"Inject it through my cranial fissures!... Soon!"

Of course! How had it not occurred to him? And the gravedigger, on his knees, injects the entire contents of the syringe into the fissures.

But surely something has gotten to the fissure that the little man desperately clings to. After eight years of abstinence, what molecule of cocaine does not ignite a delusion of strength, youth, and beauty?

The gravedigger fixed his eyes on the orbit of the skull and did not recognize the dying little man. His eyes, especially, once glassy and dull, now shone with such passion that the gravedigger had an impulse of envious surprise.

"And what about the cocaine?" He murmured.

The voice inside rang with ineffable charm.

"Ah! It is necessary to know what eight years of agony are! I've waited eight years, desperate, frozen, caught in eternity for the sole hope of a drop! Yes, it is because of the cocaine. And you? I know that smell. It's chloroform, isn't it?"

"Yes," replied the gravedigger, ashamed of the pettiness of his artificial paradise. And he added in a low voice: "Chloroform too... I would kill myself rather than leave it."

The voice sounded a bit mocking.

"Kill yourself! You would rot in three hours, you

and your wishes."

"It is true," thought the gravedigger. But the other had not given up. Even after eight years, the passion that resisted the lack of the glass of delight burned. That longing surpassed the capital death of the organism that created it. He could not eradicate the desire, as it monstrously survives from himself, transmuting the intense longing into supreme final enjoyment, remaining for eternity in the roughness of the old skull.

The warm voice, drawn with voluptuousness, still sounded mocking.

"You would kill yourself... Nice! I killed myself too. Ah, you are interested! The truth? We are of a different kind. However, bring your chloroform, and listen to me. You will then appreciate a few things."

The gravedigger returned. Lying on his chest on the ground, propped up on his elbows and the flask under his nose, waiting.

Your chlorine! It's not much, let's say. And even morphine. Do you know the love for perfumes? No? And have you heard about Jicky de Guerlain? Listen carefully, then. At thirty, I got married to a lovely woman and had three healthy creatures. She was happy. However, our house was too big for us. You have seen it. Haven't you? Well, have you seen that luxuriously set rooms seem more lonely and useless? Mostly lonely. Our entire palace thus lived in silence in pure and funerary luxury.

One day, in less than eighteen hours, our oldest son passed away due to diphtheria. The next afternoon the second one left with his brother, and my wife was desperate about the only thing we had left: our four-month-old daughter. What did we care about diphtheria, viral diseases, and everything else? Despite the doctor's order, her mother breastfed the baby, and after a while, the little girl writhed in convulsions, to die eight hours later, poisoned by her mother's milk.

Add up: 18, 24, 9. In 51 hours, just over two days, our house was completely silent because there was nothing to do. My wife was in her room, and I was walking by her side. We didn't make a sound. And just two days before, we had three children.

Well. My wife spent four days tending to the garden, and I decided to try morphine.

"Leave that," the doctor told me, "it's not for you."

"What then?" And I pointed out the funereal luxury of my home that continued to ignite catastrophes.

.

The man commiserated.

Ah, the cocaine! So many emotions fit in a single

drop of cocaine! Astonishment at having suffered immense pain, moments before; flat confidence in life, now; quick reappearance of illusions that bring the future closer to ten centimeters from the open soul, all this rushes into the veins through the platinum needle. And your chloroform!... My wife died. For two years, I spent far more on cocaine than you can imagine. Do you know anything about tolerances? Five hundred grams of morphine fatally kill a robust individual. I took two grams per day for fifteen years; that is to say, forty times more than the lethal dose.

But one has to pay the price sooner or later. In me, the truth of sad things, contained, drunk day after day, began to take revenge, and I no longer had the twisted nerves to get ahead of the horrible hallucinations that besieged me. I then made unheard-of efforts to cast out the demon, to no avail. Three times I resisted cocaine for a month, a whole month. And I relapsed. And you do not know, but you will know one day what suffering, what anguish, what a sweat of agony you feel when you try to suppress the drug for a single day!

At last, poisoned to the depths of my being, pregnant with torture and ghosts, turned into a trembling human spoil; without life—misery to which cocaine lent ten times per day a disguise, to immediately sink into a deepening stupor, at last, a remnant of dignity threw me into a sanatorium. I handed myself tied hands and feet for healing.

Under the rule of a forceful will, constantly under surveillance so that I could not get ahold of the poison, they would inevitably decocainize me.

Do you know what happened? That I, together with the heroism to give myself to torture, had a small bottle of cocaine well hidden in my pocket. Now you imagine what true passion is.

For a whole year after that failure, I kept injecting myself. As luck would have it, at this point in my life, I fell in love.

The voice fell silent. The gravedigger, who listened with the drooling smile always fixed on his face, brought his eyes close and thought he noticed a slightly opaque and glassy veil on those of his interlocutor. The complexion, in turn, was visibly cracking.

"Yes," the voice continued—"it is the beginning. I will conclude at once. To you, a colleague, I owe this whole story."

Her parents did their best to resist: a drug addict! To my fatality, hers, everyone's, I had put a super-nervous woman in my way. Oh, admirably beautiful! She was only eighteen years old. Luxury was to her what cut crystal was to an essence: her natural container.

The first time I forgot to give me a new injection before entering, she saw me fall sharply in her presence, become idiotic, her eyes huge, beautiful, and scared. Curiously frightened! She saw me, pale and without moving, take an injection. She didn't stop looking at me for the rest of the night. And behind those dilated eyes that had just seen me, I saw at the same time her neurotic defect, her uncle in the hospital, and her epileptic younger brother.

The next day I found her breathing Jicky, her favorite perfume; she had read in twenty-four hours as much as possible about hypnotics.

Now, the more two people abnormally suck the pleasures of life to understand each other intimately, the more difficult it is to obtain ordinary enjoyment. They will unite at once, excluding all other passion, to isolate themselves in the hallucinated bliss of an artificial paradise.

In twenty days, she suspended the charm of body, beauty, youth, and elegance from the intoxicating breath of perfumes. She began to live, like me with cocaine, in the delirious heaven of her Jicky.

In the end, mutual sleepwalking at her home seemed dangerous, however fleeting, and we decided to create our paradise. None better than my own house, from which I had touched nothing, and to which I had not returned. Comfortable couches abounded in the living room, and there, in the same silence and the same funeral sumptuousness that had incubated the death of my children;

in the deep stillness of the room, under the heavy atmosphere of perfumes, we lived hours and hours our quiet idyll. I lay motionless with my eyes open, pale as death; she stretched out on the couch, holding the jar of Jicky under her nose with her frozen hand.

There was no slightest trace of desire in us—and how beautiful she was with her deep dark circles, messy hairstyle, and the fiery luxury of her immaculate skirt!

For three consecutive months, I am rarely absent, without ever wondering what combinations of visits, weddings, and garden parties I should have attended so as not to arouse suspicion. On the rare occasions when I wasn't there, she would arrive the next day anxious. She would enter without looking at me. She would toss her hat with a brusque gesture to lie down immediately, her head thrown back and her eyes narrowed, at the somnambulism of her Jicky.

In short: one afternoon, and due to one of those inexplicable reactions with which the poisoned organisms explode their defense reserves—the morphine lovers know them well!—I felt all the profound enjoyment that there was, not in my cocaine, but in that body of eighteen, admirably made to be desired. That afternoon, as never before, her beauty emerged pale and sensual from the great stillness of the lighted room. So abrupt was her jerk that she found me sitting on the couch, staring at her. She was such a beautiful eighteen-year-old woman!

She saw me arrive without making a move, and as I leaned down, she looked at me with cold strangeness.

"Yes..." I murmured.

"No, no ..." she replied with a soft voice, avoiding my mouth in the heavy movement of her hair.

At last, she threw her head behind her and gave in, closing her eyes.

Ah! I was dead forever, drowned, dissolved in the sea of cocaine! I fell beside her, seated on the floor, and buried my head between her knees, thus remaining an entire hour in profound silence, while she, very pale, also remained immobile, her eyes open, fixed on the ceiling.

But that whip of reaction that had ignited a fleeting flash of sensory ruin also brought to the surface of my conscience how much masculine honor and virile shame agonized in me. My failure in the sanatorium and the diary of my dignity was nothing compared to that moment. Why live, if the artificial hell I had plunged into and from which I could not get out, was unable to absorb myself fully! And I had let go for a moment, to sink into that ending!

I got up and went inside, where I hid my revolver. When I returned, her eyelids were closed.

"Let's kill ourselves," I said.

She half-opened her eyes, and for a minute, she didn't look away from me. Her clean forehead returned to the same movement of tired ecstasy:

"Yes. Let's kill ourselves," she murmured.

At once, she glanced at the funerary luxury of the room, in which the lamp burned with high light, as she slightly rose her breast.

"Not here," she added.

We went out together, still hallucinating, and walked through the ringing house. At last, she leaned against a door and closed her eyes. She fell along the wall. An instant later, I turned the gun on myself and fired.

Then, when the explosion occurred, my jaw dropped abruptly, and I felt an immense tingling in my head. When my heart had two or three starts and stopped, paralyzed, when in my brain and my nerves and blood, there was not the remotest probability that life would return to them, I felt that I fulfilled my debt. She had killed me, but I had killed her in turn!

And I was wrong! Because an instant later, I could see, entering hesitantly and hand in hand, through the door of the room, our dead bodies, which returned stubbornly, saying:

"Cocaine, please! Give me cocaine!"

THE FEATHER PILLOW

Their honeymoon was long and chilling. Blond, angelic, and shy, her husband's tough character stopped her girly dreams of a fairy tale marriage. She loved him dearly, sometimes with a slight shiver when coming back down the street at night together while looking at Jordán's tall stature. He, for his part, loved her deeply, without showing his affections.

For three months, they—having been married in April—lived in special joy. Without a doubt, she would have wanted less seriousness in that rigid sky of love, but her husband's impassive countenance always stopped her.

The house they lived in was big and cold. The whiteness of the silent courtyard—marble friezes, columns, and statues—produced an autumn impression of an enchanted palace. Inside, the icy sheen of the stucco, without the slightest scratch on the high walls, affirmed that feeling of unpleasant cold. As they crossed from one room to another, the footsteps echoed throughout the house.

In that strange love nest, Alicia spent the whole fall. However, she had ended up casting a veil over her old dreams. She lived carefree in that hostile house, not wanting to think about anything until her husband arrived.

It was not uncommon for her to lose weight. She had a slight bout of the flu that dragged on insidiously for days that Alicia didn't seem to overcome. Finally, one afternoon she was able to go out into the garden leaning on the arm of her beloved. She looked indifferently from one side to the other. Suddenly, Jordán passed his hand over her head with profound tenderness, and Alicia immediately broke into sobs, throwing her arms around his neck. She wept for a long time, talking about all her silent terrors, doubling her tears at the slightest attempt at a caress. Then, the sobs slowed down. She remained hidden in his neck for a long time, without moving or saying a word.

That was the last day Alicia was up. The next day she woke up feeling tired and in pain, unable to get on her feet. Jordán's doctor examined her carefully, ordering her absolute rest.

"I don't know," the doctor told Jordán at the front door, his voice still low. "She is frail, and I can't explain why. There's no vomit, nothing. If she wakes up tomorrow like today, call me right away."

The next day Alicia was still worse. Jordán called the doctor immediately. He discovered that Alicia was suffering from an acute case of anemia, completely unexplainable given her lifestyle. Alicia no longer fainted but was visibly on her way to the grave. For most of the day, the bedroom was with the lights on and in complete silence. Hours went by without hearing the slightest noise. Alicia was often asleep. Jordán spent almost every moment in the living room, also with all the lights on. He walked endlessly around the room with tireless obstinacy. The carpet silenced his steps. From time to time, he would go into the bedroom and continue his mute swaying along the bed, glancing at his wife every time he walked in her direction.

Soon, Alicia began to hallucinate. With her eyes wide open, the young woman continuously looked at the carpet on both sides of the bed. One night she was suddenly staring at a spot in her living room. After a while, she opened her mouth to scream.

"Jordán! Jordán!" she cried, stiff with horror, still staring at the carpet.

Jordán ran to the bedroom, and when Alicia saw him appear, she screamed in horror.

"Alicia! It's just me!"

Alicia looked at him confusedly, looked at the carpet, looked at him again, and after a long time of confusion, she calmed down. She smiled and took her husband's hand between hers, trembling.

Among her most stubborn hallucinations, an anthropoid was leaning on the carpet on its fingers, staring at her.

The doctors returned to no avail. There was a life in front of them that was ending, bleeding day by day, hour by hour, without knowing quite how. At the last consultation, Alicia lay in a stupor while they checked her pulse, passing her inert wrist from one end to the other. They watched her for a long time in silence and then walked to the dining room.

"Pst ..." his doctor shrugged, discouraged. "It is a serious case. There is little to do."

"That's all I needed!" Jordán snorted as he drummed nervously on the table.

Alicia looked worse and worse in her delirium of anemia, aggravated late in the day, but which always remitted in the first hours. During the day, her illness did not progress, but every morning she woke up worse. It seemed that only at night was her life slowly lost. When she woke up, she always felt slumped in bed with a massive weight on top. From the third day onwards, this horrible feeling never left her. She could barely move her head. She did not want her bed touched or even her pillow fixed. Her twilight terrors advanced in the form of monsters that crawled to her mattress and crept towards her.

Then she lost consciousness. The final two days, she raved incessantly in a low voice. The lights were still fiercely turned on in the bedroom and living room. In the unbearable silence of the house, nothing was heard except the monotonous delirium coming out of the bed and the muffled sound of the eternal footsteps of Jordán.

Alicia died, finally. The maid, who came in later to undo the bed, already alone, took a long look at the pillow in surprise.

"Sir!" she called to Jordán in a low voice. "There are stains on the pillow. They look like blood!"

Jordán approached quickly and took a long, hard look. Indeed, on the cover, on both sides of the spot where Alicia's head stood, there were dark spots.

"They look like bites," the maid murmured after a while of motionless observation.

"Hold it up to the light," Jordán told her.

The maid picked it up but immediately dropped it and stared at it, livid and trembling. Without knowing why, Jordán felt his hair stand on end.

"What's in there?"

"It's cumbersome!" the maid said while trembling.

On the dining room table, Jordán cut the pillow's wrap. Jordán picked it up; it was extraordinary in weight. He carried it and left the room. The upper feathers flew, and the servant girl gave an open-mouthed cry of horror, clasping her clenched hands to the sides. On the bottom of the feathers, slowly moving its hairy legs, was a monstrous animal, a living, slimy ball. It was so swollen that its mouth was barely visible.

Night after night, since Alicia had fallen into bed, it had stealthily attached its mouth to her temples, sucking her blood. The sting was almost invisible. The daily removal of the pillow had undoubtedly impeded its development, but ever since the young woman could no longer move, the suction was constant. In just five nights, it had emptied Alicia.

These parasites of birds, tiny in their familiar environment, acquire enormous proportions under certain conditions. Human blood seems particularly favorable to them, and it is not uncommon to find them on feather pillows.

THE DEAD MAN

The man had just cleared the banana plantation's fifth road using his machete. He needed to clear two more roads, but as they were abundant with sticks and wild hollyhocks, the task ahead was quite simple. Consequently, the man took a satisfied look towards the bushes, crossing the fence to lie down on the grass for a while.

As his body passed the barbed wire, his left foot slipped on a piece of bark detached from the post, just as the machete slipped from his hand. As he fell, the man had the extremely distant impression of not seeing the machete fall flat on the ground.

He was lying on the grass, on his right side, just as he wanted. He was lying down comfortably, his knees bent and his left hand on his chest. Behind his forearm and immediately below his belt, the first half of the machete blade emerged from his shirt, but the rest of it was not visible.

The man tried to shake his head in vain. He cast a sideways glance at the hilt of the machete, still damp from the sweat on his hand. He acknowledged the extension and trajectory of the machete inside his belly and acquired the cold, mathematical and inexhaustible assurance that he had just reached the end of his existence.

Death: In the course of life, it's common to think that one day, after years, months, weeks, and days, we will arrive in our turn at the threshold of death. It is the fatal law, accepted and foreseen, so much so that we tend to let imagination take pleasure of that moment, supreme among all when we take our last breath. But between the present moment and that final expiration, what dreams, upheavals, hopes, and dramas we boast in our lives! What does this vigorous existence still have in store for us before eliminating us from the human scene! Death is so far away and so unforeseen that we must still live! Still...?

Not two seconds have passed: the sun is precisely at the same height; the shadows haven't advanced an inch. Abruptly, the ramblings have just dissipated for the man: he is dying. He can be considered dead in his comfortable posture. But the man opens his eyes and looks. How much time has passed? What cataclysm has survived in the world?

He is going to die. Coldly, fatally and inescapably, he is going to die.

The man resists—the horror of death is so unexpected—and thinks: This is just a nightmare! And he looks ahead: Isn't that the banana plantation? Does he not come every morning to clean it? Who knows it as well as he does? He sees the banana plantation perfectly, very bright, with the broad bare leaves under the sun. But now they are not moving. Through the bananas, the man sees the red roof of his house. To the left, he glimpses at the mountain. He can't see more, but he knows very well that behind him is the road to the new port and that, down there, lies at the bottom of the valley, the Paraná River asleep like a lake. Everything else is the same as always: the fiery sun, the vibrant and lonely air, the immobile bananas, and the very thick and tall wire fence.

Dead! But is it possible? Isn't this one of the many days he has left home at dawn with a machete in hand? Isn't the horse right there, forty feet from him, his Malacara, sniffing the barbed wire? Yes, of course!

Someone whistles. The man cannot see because his back is to the road, but he hears a horse's footsteps drawing nearer. The boy passes through every morning to the new port at eleven-thirty, always whistling. From the post that almost reaches his boots to the mountain fence separating the banana plantation from the road, there's a distance of fifty feet, which he measured when he built it.

What's the matter, then? Is it not just another ordinary noon of the many in Misiones, on its mountain, in its pasture, in the sparse banana plantation? Definitely! Short grass, ant cones, silence, hot sun. Nothing, absolutely nothing has changed. Only he is different. For two minutes, his person has nothing to do with either the paddock, which he built himself or the banana plantation, the works of his own hands. Nor with his family. His life has been roughly torn off, naturally, by the result of a machete to the belly.

The man, very tired and lying on the grass on his right side, is always reluctant to admit a phenomenon of this transcendence, given the ordinary and monotonous aspect of everything he sees. He knows the time well: eleven-thirty. The boy has just crossed the bridge.

But slipping is impossible...! He held the machete handle (he will soon have to exchange it for another as it's already very worn out) firmly between his left hand and the barbed wire. After ten years in the forest, he knows very well how to handle a bush machete. He was exhausted from work that morning and rested for a while as usual. There's the grass that now enters through the corner of his mouth, planted by him. And there's the Malacara, standing still, as usual. He sees everything perfectly; he knows that the Malacara doesn't dare to turn the corner of the fence because he is lying almost at the foot of the post. The sun is beating down, and the calm is significant because not a fringe of the bananas moves. Every day he has seen the same things.

He was exhausted, resting alone. It must have been several minutes since the incident. From the chalet with the red roof, his wife and his two sons will come off to the banana plantation to look for him for lunch at a quarter to twelve. He always hears the voice of his youngest boy first, who wants to let go of the hand of his mother: "¡Father! Father!"

He hears the voice of his son. What a nightmare! But it is one of many days, trivial as all, of course! Excessive light and yellowish shadows make the Malacara sweat before the dying man.

Very tired, but nothing more. How many times, at noon like now, has he crossed that pasture, returning home, which was a small grazing field when he arrived so many years ago. He would then return slowly, exhausted, with his machete hanging from his left hand. He can still walk away with his mind if he wants to; he can leave his body for a moment and see from the roof he built the usual trivial landscape: the volcanic gravel with rigid grass, the banana plantation, and its red sand. And at the foot of a chipped post, lying on his right side and his legs folded up, exactly like every day, he can see himself, as a small sunny bundle on the grass—resting because he is exhausted.

The horse, streaked with sweat and motionless with caution before the corner of the fence, sees the man on the ground and does not dare to cross the banana plantation. Ahead of the voices already close by—"Papa!"—the horse turns around. Finally reassured, the Malacara decided to pass between the post and the lying man, already dead.

THE SON

It is a powerful summer day in Misiones, with all the sun, heat, and calm that the season can bring.

"Be careful, little one," the father says to his son, abridging in that sentence all the past experiences that his son remembers.

"Yes, Papa," the creature replies as he takes the shotgun and loads the pockets of his shirt with cartridges, which he closes carefully.

"Come back for lunch," the father said.

"Yes, Papa," the boy repeats.

He balances the shotgun in his hand, smiles at his father, kisses him on the head, and departs. His father follows him for a while with his eyes and goes back to work.

He knows that since he brought up his son from his earliest childhood in habit and caution from danger, his son can handle a rifle and hunt anywhere he wants. Although he is very tall for his age, he is only thirteen years old; he seems to be younger, with childish surprise judging by his blue eyes' purity.

He has crossed the red trail and is heading straight up the mountain through the open plains.

Hunting in the bush—fur game—requires more patience than his son can yield. After crossing that mountain, his son will go along the edge of the cacti searching for pigeons or toucans, such as those his friend Juan found days before. They only sometimes hunt crows—even less often—and they return in triumph, Juan to his ranch with the nine-millimeter rifle that his father has given him, and his son to the plateau with the great Saint-Étienne shotgun, 16 gauge, quadruple lock, and white powder. Only now, the father smiles at the memory of the passion for hunting of the two creatures.

He was the same. At thirteen, he would have given his life to own a shotgun. His son, of that age, owns it now, and the father smiles.

However, it is not easy for a widowed father, with no other faith or hope than the life of his son, to educate him as he has done, sure of his little hands and feet since he was four years old, aware of the immensity of certain dangers.

The boy's father had to fight hard against what he considered pure selfishness. It happens so quickly; a father miscalculates, allows a child to do something reckless, and loses a child!

The danger always exists for a man at any age, but the threat diminishes if he grows accustomed to having nothing to count on but his strength. In this way, the father has correctly educated his son. And to achieve this, he had to resist not only his heart but his moral torments; because the father, with a weak stomach and eyes, has been suffering from hallucinations.

He has seen, embodied in the most painful illusion, memories of happiness that should have existed had his wife not died. The image of his son has not escaped this torment. He had once hallucinated seeing him roll wrapped in blood when the boy fired the shotgun in his workshop, being so what he did was to work on the buckle of his hunting belt.

Horrible, horrible. But today, on this burning summer day, the father, who deeply loves his son, feels happy, calm, and assured of the future.

At that moment, not far away, he hears a boom.

"The Saint-Étienne shotgun," murmurs the father, recognizing the detonation—"two fewer pigeons in the bush."

Paying no more attention to the inconsequential event, the man absorbs himself again in his task.

The sun, already high, continues to climb.

Wherever one looks—stones, earth, trees—the rarefied air as a furnace vibrates with heat. A deep hum that permeates the area as far as the eye can see concentrates all tropical life at that time.

The father glances at his wrist: twelve. Then he lifts his eyes to the mountain, thinking that his son should be back by now. In the mutual trust they place in each other—the silver-tempted father and the thirteen-year-old child—they never deceive each other. When the son responds to him: "Yes, Dad," he will do what he says. He said that he would be back before twelve, and the father smiled when he saw him leave. And he has not returned.

The man goes back to his work, trying to focus his attention on his task. Is it so easy to lose track of time inside the forest and sit on the ground while resting motionless?

More time has passed; it is half-past twelve. The father leaves his workshop, and as he rests his hand on the mechanical bench, the explosion of a parabellum bullet rises from the depths of his memory. Instantly, for the first time, he thinks that after the explosion of the Saint-Étienne, he has not heard anything. His son has not returned, and nature is stopped at the edge of the forest, waiting for him.

Oh! A temperate character and a blind trust in a child's education are not enough to chase away the specter of doom that a father with sick eyes sees rising from the mountain line. Distraction, forgetfulness, fortuitous delay: none of these small reasons that could delay the arrival of his child found a place in his heart.

One shot, he only heard one shot, and it was a long time ago. Besides it, the father has not heard a noise, has not seen a bird or has not seen a single person come to announce a great misfortune.

Head in the air, and without a machete, the father goes. He enters the mountain, coasts the line of cacti without finding the slightest trace of his son.

But nature goes unopposed. And when the father has walked the familiar hunting trail, he acquires the assurance that every step he takes after that leads him, fatally and inevitably, to the corpse of his son.

Reproaching didn't do him any good. Only the cold, terrible, and consumed reality: his son has died somewhere. But where? There are so many fields there, and the mountain is so, so rocky! Oh, very rocky! His son might not have been careful when crossing a barbed wire with the shotgun in his hand.

The father stifles a cry. He has seen something rise in the distance. Oh, it is not his son, no! He then turns to another side, and another and another.

He would gain nothing by seeing the color of his complexion and the anguish in his eyes. Although his heart cries out for him, his mouth remains mute. He knows well that the very act of pronouncing the name will be the confession of his death.

"My son!"—Suddenly escapes him. And if the voice of a man of character is capable of crying, let us cover our ears with mercy before the anguish that one could hear in the father's voice.

No one and nothing answered. Through the red bites of the sun, the father goes looking for his son, who, he presumes, has just died.

"My son ...! My little boy..!" He calls out in a diminutive that rises from the bottom of his insides.

Some time ago, in complete happiness and peace, the father had suffered the hallucination of his son rolling with his forehead open by a nickel-chrome bullet. Now, in every shadowy corner of the forest, he sees flashes of wire; and at the foot of a pole, he sees something with the unloaded shotgun beside him.

"My son!"

The forces that allow a poor hallucinating father to participate in the most heinous nightmare also have limits. And it feels that those forces are evading him when he abruptly sees his son in the distance, sitting next to the barbed wire.

It is enough for a thirteen-year-old boy to see his father's expression inside the mountain to hasten his step with wet eyes from fifty meters.

"My son..." the man murmurs. And, exhausted, he collapses, sitting on the sloping sand, wrapping his arms around the legs of his son.

The creature remains standing; and as he understands his father's pain, he slowly caresses his head:

"Poor dad."

"It's getting late. It is going to be three o'clock. We should head back." said the father.

Together now, father and son walk hastily towards their house.

"What were you thinking? How did you not look at the sun to know the time ...?" The father murmurs still.

"I noticed, papa ... But when I was going to return, I saw Juan's herons, and I followed them ..."

"Think about what you put me through, little one!"

"Dad ..." the boy also murmurs.

After a long silence:

"And the pigeons, did you kill them?" Asked the

father.

"No."

Insignificant detail, after all. Under the red-hot sky and air, the man returns home with his son, on whose shoulders, almost as high as his own, the happy arms of his father swing forcefully. He returns drenched in sweat, and though broken in body and soul, he smiles with happiness.

He smiles in temporary happiness since the father walks alone.

He has found no one, and his arms rest in the void. Deep in the field, at the foot of a post, tangled in the barbed wire, his beloved son lies in the sun, dead since ten in the morning.

THE ARTIFICIAL MAN

The rat lay motionless, upside down, between Donissoff's white hands. The three men, holding their breaths, bent over the animal lying on the table.

"And...?" Ortiz exclaimed eagerly.

Donissoff took a while to answer. The angelic beauty of his face had taken on an implacable tone.

"Nothing, yet," he finally answered. "It is not time yet."

Suddenly a fleeting flash crossed his pupils.

"The rat's temperature is dropping! What should we do, Ortiz?"

Ortiz ran to the laboratory and activated the electrical switch. Donissoff's gaze never left the thermometer suspended in front of the table.

"Is it going up?" Ortiz yelled from the other room.

"Yes ... 39° ... 39.1° ... 39.3° ... Enough"

Ortiz returned immediately. Meanwhile, the rat, the immeasurable concern of the three men, remained motionless. Two large tables held the most sophisticated chemistry, anatomy, and bacteriology equipment available. In the immense laboratory, most of it in darkness, except for the eight electric lamps with green shades that cast their light on the table, the three experimenters looked unusual and even gloomy, bent and with their souls in suspense, over a simple rat. The heat was suffocating, but they didn't seem to notice. Moreover, bending over the animal, they continued to devour the filthy rat in Donissoff's hands with their eyes.

"Sivel, the syringe! The reaction is about to begin!" Donissoff suddenly exclaimed. Sivel jumped up, picked up the requested object from the table, and handed it to the young sage, holding the rat's head in his hands. Cold, despite the immense boiling of his soul, Donissoff injected the animal with the red liquid from the syringe.

Ten seconds, fifteen, twenty, a minute passed. What those three men felt in that endless time is difficult to appreciate. Not one spoke; no one moved; they barely blinked. So when Donissoff's voice broke the tragic silence, something like an immense sigh lifted all three souls.

"It moves ..." Donissoff said, whose hand, placed on the rat's heart, trembled.

His voice was trembling too. Sivel and Ortiz, their faces radiant by the most violent emotion, looked at each other. Then it was true! They, only they, had done the impossible! All the work, all the horrible worries of those three years vanished forever. And it was the work of the three of them, not one, but all of them!

They bent over the rat again and stood still while Donissoff's slender hand continued over its beating heart.

"Go on ..." Donissoff murmured after a long moment. "Let's hope for more ..."

They waited yet another endless minute. Then, at last, Donissoff's hand slowly moved away from the rat's heart. He raised his face transfigured with emotion, in which his eyes shone with the most incredible pride that can fit in a human gaze, and with a clear voice, he said to his companions:

"It's been two minutes. The blood cells are alive. The rat is alive."

Then they witnessed the most amazing thing imaginable.

He climbed onto the table with one leap and danced the most disorderly dance of the possible and impossible worlds. Immediately he flung himself to the floor and wrapped himself in the linoleum, spinning around. From there came his hoarse voice which said:

"Hurray for Donissoff! Hooray for Sivel! Hooray for Ortiz!"

At last, the mad delirium subsided, and Donissoff felt exhausted.

In the meantime, Sivel smiled at the tiny rat. Donissoff, sitting at a table with his knees between his arms, stood motionless, his eyes lost.

As often happens, the formidable feat that Donissoff just accomplished, thanks to his genius and with the help of his companions, only reminded him of all the failures of his previous work. In addition, his nerves, capable of withstanding a very high tension, were also exposed to falling into equivalent exhaustion.

"Well, Donissoff," Sivel said, putting his hand affectionately on his shoulder.

"I'm exhausted; I'm thirsty. Let's rest for a while. Do you know what time it is?"

"It's four! And we haven't sat down since six in the morning. And that character," he added, turning sideways to the rat lying on its back, "begins its initiation into life with a good dream ... But I'm not hungry; only thirsty."

"I would have tea," Ortiz said. "But on the condition that Donissoff comes."

"Donissoff ...?"

"Come on," he said, and the three subjects who had associated their profound scientific capacity, the three magicians whom the Inquisition would have burned three hundred years earlier without wasting a second, collapsed on the dining room.

These three individuals who had just "created" a living being were named Nicolás Ivanovich Donissoff, Luigi Marco Sivel, and Ricardo Ortiz.

Donissoff was Russian and the last descendant of one of the noblest families from the old Russian Empire.

He lost his parents when he was still very young, and an old family friend, Prince Dolgorouky, was entrusted with his education and the administration of his immense fortune.

Donissoff grew up in an atmosphere of deep adherence to the czar. His family, from time immemorial, had been intimately involved in the administration of the Muscovite empire. Among the recent upheavals, the czar counted with the support of Donissoff's father. As a result, the boy had a deep reverence for all that belonged to the Russian government. He lived under the autocracy atmosphere, which lasted until the young man was eighteen years old. At that time, reading aroused certain feelings in him, making him see things differently and wholly transforming his spirit.

One night, early in the morning, Prince Dolgorouky, returning from a reception at the palace, was surprised to see a reflection coming from the ward's room. He entered it and found Donissoff lying on the bed, still dressed in a tailcoat, reading one of those books that cost the writer's neck.

Fifteen days later, secret police officers caught Donissoff in a cafe frequented by revolutionaries. If it had been any other nobleman, the young man would have ended his days in Siberia, but that faith was not possible for the son of Alexis Donissoff.

Nevertheless, counterclaims rained down on him, and even Grand Duke Ivan plotted to stop him one afternoon as he was leaving the palace.

"Take great care!" Said Grand Luke Ivan, smiling. "Remember another prince like you, who has also written books like the one you read."

The Grand Duke alluded to Prince Kropotkin.

"I don't know what book Your Highness is referring to," Donissoff replied, flushing.

The Grand Duke looked at him carefully.

"Why are you lying, prince?" He told him.

"Pardon Your Highness; I'm not lying," Donissoff said, blushing and outrage burning his face.

This time the Grand Duke took pity on him, and with a new smile, he gently nudged him by the shoulder.

"Good, Nicolas Ivanovich. Don't read those books, and don't go to those cafes, even if you've never been there. Stay in peace."

For days Donissoff felt remorse for his lie.

He felt debased, mainly because he lied out of fear. "I was afraid to tell them the truth; I am a coward," he told himself, "a miserable coward. I was afraid to say that I read a book!"

At the end of those ten days, Donissoff had a meeting with his tutor, whom he loved dearly. As a consequence of it, Donissoff renounced the prerogatives of his position and his immense fortune. And if a curious person had looked, six months later, into an icy garret in the seediest neighborhood of Saint Petersburg, he would have seen a young man, shivering with hunger and a shortage of clothes, elbows on his medical books.

To live, he loaded trunks at the station; months later, he was cleaning tubes in a bacteriology institute, and being the genius who was beginning to have great ideas in his mind, he soon became a teacher. Soon afterward, he became the head of the famous institute.

Like many others who have lost their rightful inheritance, he would go to his former palace in disguise from time to time. Meanwhile, he continued his academic studies, at the same time frequenting the revolutionaries. The violent feelings of justice did not take long to bring him to the most advanced ranks. When in January 1902, the Central Committee of the Russian Revolution discussed the death of Prince Dolgorouky, Donissoff denounced the influence of another prince as direr. No one was unaware of the awe Donissoff had, pure and unsullied, for the old prince.

Hearing it, his companions froze for a moment; the greatness of that sacrifice escaped no one.

"I think," someone said after a moment, "that Galitzine's influence is greater."

"I don't think so," Donissoff said.

"I am well informed," argued the first.

"And I'm sure of it."

The other looked at him for a long time.

"But you love him very much ..."

"Immensely," Donissoff said, deathly pale.

His companions lowered their heads to avoid seeing two tears, tears of blood, tears arising from the depths of a soul burned in justice that rolled down Donissoff's cheeks.

Everyone remembers the five shots fired in the chest at Prince Dolgorouky on January 11, 1903, as he left the Supreme Court. Donissoff spent the entire day of the attack in his room, not wanting to see anyone. He was immediately arrested and did not want to answer a word, determined to spend the rest of his life in Siberia. But his companions forced him to escape.

Donissoff spent a year in Vienna devoted with all his soul to his scientific experiments. Then, from Vienna, he went to Paris, staying in that capital for three years.

If he had been older, perhaps a new explosion of love for those who suffer would have extinguished the pain of that wound. But at twenty-three, the fibers of the heart lack sufficient thickness to withstand vibrations of that kind, and thus Donissoff was wounded forever. Yes, he recovered his will and indomitable energy; but he could not return to Russia. Then his mature genius absorbed or at least directed his other faculties. So he studied for another year in London, and at the end of 1905, he arrived in Buenos Aires.

Stefano Marco Sivel was Italian from an impoverished family. His father, a former Calabrian bandit, who had abandoned his profession because of a broken arm, exercised the same disciplinary habits with his son that he had with his comrades. As a result, little Marco suffered the most horrendous beatings possible to receive without dying, and he knew the real meaning of hunger, locked in a cellar black as night, soaked with water, and riddled with rats. The reason: there was little that Marco earned by begging on the street in the middle of winter, wearing a ripped shirt.

Later, when he was old enough to arouse lucrative pity, his father had him instructed by an old bandit like himself in the art of tour guiding. Little Marco learned in two or three hours as much as the robber knew about ruins and Roman history and a great deal more on his own. But what Little Marco did not learn was to practice robbery. He believed himself the happiest of mortals if some traveler gave him a lyre.

On these occasions, as on all occasions, his father seized the money. But, when the profit was nil, the old bandit went into a dark fury, and the blows from a closed fist rained down on the creature's mouth.

As his son never complained, the father believed that he did not feel the blows and, consequently, had the idea of sending him to find a wire and, hanging it from the ceiling, he would whip his body with that dreadful instrument.

"How much?" Asked the old man.

"A lyre."

"Give it to me," he held out his hand.

The next day:

"How much?"

"Nothing"

"Okay: go get the wire."

It was always a new wire that the creature had to fetch from the stream. Marco would return after a while with the instrument of torture only to remove his clothes without a sigh.

Time went by like this, and Marco became twelve years old. Then, one afternoon the usual dialogue started again.

"How much?"

"Nothing."

"Okay: go get the wire."

"No," said the boy.

His father abruptly turned.

"What did you say?"

"Nothing, I'm not going to look for the wire."

Slowly the father got up. Step by step, he approached his son until he was almost touching his face. His face went livid as a blue ray crossed his old robber's eyes.

"You say you're not going to look for the wire?"

"No," Marco said without moving, as pale as his father. The old man gazed at him for a while without moving a single muscle. It was no longer lightning that crossed his eyes but a sinister light that was growing.

"Go get the wire!" He roared livid now with fury.

"No," the creature replied again as he closed his eyes. When he opened them, his father, hideously livid, took off his cap.

"Okay," he hissed. "Stay, I'll go."

When he returned, the creature was sitting at the table, his head thrown on his arms.

His father touched him lightly on the shoulder.

"Get naked!"

"No, father!" Marco replied without raising his head.

"Madonna! Light, light! Get naked!" The old man exploded, at last, making the table jump with a fist.

"No," the boy still answered. And with his arms crossed, he closed his eyes as if he were dying, and he thought of his mother: "Mom ... Mom, dear mom!"

A moment passed, another. There was not the slightest noise. Trembling, Marco raised his head and saw his father, still standing, staring at him. The old bandit's hand fell slowly on the boy's shoulder.

"Okay," he said hoarsely. Okay, you are my son; I recognize my blood. You are worthy, my son. But..." he added, turning even more livid, "get out of here forever because I would smash your head against the wall. No one in the world has done in front of me what you just did. You are my son. I recognize you. But go right away! Never set foot here again!"

And he threw his son out into the street.

After his first months of freedom—the freedom of a hungry creature, without a home and affection of any kind—Marco was fortunate that a carpenter took him as an apprentice. Between strokes of the brush and the turn of the drill, he fortified his desire for study.

He studied at night while he ate, still in the workshop. His dedication elicited the affection of the teacher, who taught him many things. Later, with another job, he completed High School, soon entering the Faculty of Medicine with very high marks.

After fifteen years, no one named a medical celebrity without Sivel's name emerging with all the brilliance of his great halo. At this time, his heart, hitherto asleep, was kindled in passionate love for a young woman who, in turn, had given him her entire soul. The courtship ran in the greatest happiness until one morning; another young woman arrived at his clinic in the hospital, whom an intense hemorrhage had deprived of almost all the blood. At night he told his girlfriend about the case.

"She's a poor girl who needs a lot of blood. If by tomorrow she does not improve, it will be necessary to undergo a transfusion."

His girlfriend, who knew him well, made him swear through a sea of tears that he would not give the girl a single drop of his blood.

"I won't love you anymore, I swear!" She sobbed. "I swear if you do that, I won't love you anymore!"

But the following day, Sivel delivered waves of his blood to the veins of agony. He made a regrettable oversight, and Sivel fell to his bed with a terrible infection.

That afternoon, his girlfriend, still unaware, wrote to him that if he donated a single drop of blood, she would forget him forever. Sivel replied, "Do it. Besides, I'm dying."

His girlfriend never saw him again. Sivel spent two months between life and death, and when he got up, turned into a specter, horribly disfigured by the tumors that had eaten his face. The young woman, overcome by sobs, fell to her knees before him. It was the young woman from the hospital, whose romantic and tender soul felt upon hearing this an immense gratitude towards the poor man who had sacrificed his happiness to give life to someone else. Her gratitude had transformed very soon to the most extreme love.

The young woman, convulsing, pressed her mouth to Sivel's hand, but he withdrew it sharply.

"Stop! Stand up!" He said. Deep in his heart, the great wound of his love reopened before that bitterly evocative presence.

"Forgiveness! Forgiveness...!" The young woman sobbed, still on her knees.

"I have nothing to forgive you for," Sivel had the strength to smile.

"No, no ... I'm to blame ..."

Sivel then had the feeling that an indifferent hand, any hand, was clawing at his heart.

"Forgiveness...! It was my fault...! It was for me..."

"Oh no! I beg your pardon," Sivel exclaimed. "I didn't do it for you."

The young woman's eyes slowly lifted to Sivel.

"Yes, I didn't do it for you; I felt sorry for this being, for an existence condemned to die, like yours, well ... but not for you. Oh no!"

When hope of love, logical or not, is broken; When we fall from the height of a dream of greatness, such as the one that consists in having believed ourselves to inspire a great sacrifice, the fall is always terrible.

The young woman, her wild eyes fixed on that specter, also of her love, got up.

She stepped back to the door, and before Sivel could fully realize the despair that engulfed that soul, the young woman disappeared.

Shaken thus in the deepest fibers of his being, Sivel considered his life broken forever. He spent fifteen days locked up in the laboratory, wandering in semi-darkness from one place to another.

Determined at last to forget about it, his passion for science caught up with him again, this time with immense ardor. It seemed that all his faculties had been violently reborn oriented towards anatomical studies. But, as despite everything, his disfigured face made his stay in Rome hateful, he left the Eternal City, arriving in Buenos Aires in 1904.

Ricardo Ortiz was Argentine and had been born in the capital. His family, of considerable fortune, oriented him to study electrical engineering, for which Ortiz showed a strong inclination from a very young age. He did his studies in Buffalo with brilliant success.

He returned to Buenos Aires, and instead of practicing his profession, he dedicated himself to the study of electric batteries; he believed he was on the trail of a new element of astonishing intensity and consistency. However, as he did not frequent the outside world and was clumsy with his hands, his family considered that he would do very little with his career, despite his knowledge. Consequently, the father informed him that either he was leaving his line of work or he would deprive him of his monthly alimony. Ortiz opted to keep working with batteries and suddenly found himself on the street. Since he was not a businessman, he volunteered as an English and mathematics teacher the next day. His family found this wrong, and the father went to see him.

"What are you going to do with that? It's a shame for an engineer like you!"

"Maybe," Ortiz said calmly. "I will continue working."

"In there?" He pointed contemptuously to the workshop.

"Yes, there."

"We'll see! If I may propose something ..."

"Don't propose anything to me; I won't accept."

"And are you going to do that all your life?"

"Yes, all my life."

"Inventing, huh?"

"Yes."

"But you're going to dishonor us all with your failure!" Exclaimed the indignant father.

"Hey," Ortiz stared at him, "You shouldn't have come if you're just going to tell me these things."

"You embarrass me!"

"I'm embarrassed too!"

"About what?"

"About your shame! It's over! I'm not asking for a penny, and I want you to leave me alone."

His father, then, deeply irritated, threw him pointing to the workshop:

"To have so much pride, you could abandon this too because you didn't buy this workshop with your money."

"Perfect," Ortiz said, "you did well to remind me. I'm leaving here tomorrow."

"Very well, that's what you should have done a long time ago," the father replied, growing increasingly irritated. "But don't even think about coming back …!"

"Will you go, please?" Ortiz snapped, livid.

The following day Ortiz sent his father, along with the keys, the inventory of the entire workshop.

A week later, a cousin of Ortiz finally found his new address.

"I finally find you! You no longer have the workshop, do you?"

"I don't have it."

"And what are you going to do?"

"I don't know yet."

"Do you know what I would do? I would speak to your father …"

Ortiz, who imagined that his father sent his cousin, stopped him, putting his hand on his shoulder:

"Look, if you were someone else, I would have asked you to leave already. I don't want to remember anything!"

The cousin stood up hastily.

"Hey? What…?"

"If you weren't also an idiot, I'd slap you out of

here. Outside!"

A year later, Ortiz's father died, and the son renounced all his rights: an immense fortune.

Thus, these three men of character had united their energies, associating them to lend each other strength. In such circumstances, they performed the highest work of genius: to make a living being.

For the laboratory, assembled with the perfect types of machines and instruments that they expressly ordered from the United States, Sivel had given his entire fortune.

Ortiz cooperated in the everyday work with his knowledge of chemistry, Sivel with his anatomical wisdom, and Donissoff with his bacteriological knowledge.

Despite the magnificent laboratory and talents of the three associates, the enterprise was highly challenging. More than once, Donissoff, Sivel, and Ortiz fell for weeks into the most profound hopelessness.

"It's impossible, Donissoff!" Ortiz cried, throwing his test tubes on the table.

"Let's work, Ortiz," he answered without raising his head.

"We are tempting God or the devil with this!" We are not going to accomplish anything.

"If it were only about God, I wouldn't be upset," Sivel explained. "What concerns me is that we tempt the devil."

Ortiz was back at work. But at other times, it was his turn to encourage one of his colleagues. Thus they supported each other until the three of them, faced with new and insurmountable difficulties, threw everything away and closed the laboratory.

Their work lasted three years. Carbon, hydrogen, oxygen, all the primordial elements of the cell passed successively through the Ortiz electrolysis, the Sivel dissections, and the Donissoff reagents. Sometimes the conquest of three or four fundamental elements took weeks. Others, a single step forward, took up to a year. In this way, they could obtain the blood and its globules from May to September, taking instead eighteen months to conquer the hair bulb. Until August 23, 1909, three years minus twelve days after the project started, the rat came to life under the Donissoff injection.

And now, let's go back to the dining room, where the three associates, dead with satisfaction and fatigue, were resting.

"At last, it was time," Ortiz groaned, leaning back full length on a couch. "If this took ten more days, I would just prefer to die."

"Yes, I was tired too, much more than I was

letting on," Donissoff supported, serving his companions the tea that he, in his Russian character, prepared with great neatness.

"Yeah, but we made the rat," Sivel concluded.

"And now that I remember," Ortiz exclaimed, raising himself on one elbow, "why did I come up with a rat? We could have done anything else."

"Sivel chose the rat," Donissoff said.

"Yes," Sivel said, sipping his tea, "I found out about the great similarity between human and rat blood. Something I discovered by chance, many years ago, in an analysis."

"For real, Sivel?" Said Ortiz, raising his head. "And why is it not equal to that of the donkey?"

"That's a question to be asked of a donkey, you wise electrician. And you, who believe that donkey's milk is similar to that of women, why do you doubt my decision?"

"I have no doubts, professor; I am amazed and humbled."

"Are you sure, Sivel, of your analyzes?" Donissoff interrupted, who for a moment had been looking thoughtfully at the glass in the door.

"Completely. Why?"

"Because it's occurring to me," he answered

without taking his eyes off the glass, "that we could make a man."

Ortiz sat bolt upright, fixing his wide eyes on Donissoff. He scratched a nail for a long time.

"It would be much more work," Donissoff continued, his voice always lost, "but we could do it. It's possible, yes."

"Man or woman, Donissoff?"

"Man, Ortiz."

Sivel raised his eyes at last, and his gaze cast a glow of grim severity on that misshapen face that had once shone with manly beauty.

"I think it's going to be difficult," he murmured.

"Can it be done?" Ortiz asked him, sitting up correctly this time.

"I don't know ... but the work is going to break us. I already thought about that when we started creating the rat. I didn't tell you anything, out of the same fear that I have now, that we will not finish the work. It will breathe, it will digest, it will see, it will move. And you understand that doing that alone would be an eternal shame for us."

"And he will think," Ortiz replied.

"No, not that. We will give the man all his senses, good nerve transmission, good transforming brain, and no matter how many feelings he has, he will not have a single perception."

"A matter of soul, then?" Ortiz scoffed.

"No, electrician; It is not a question of the soul but inheritance. No matter how vivid the sensations are, the brain will lack the habit of perceiving, first, and not confuse the sensations later. The same thing happens with your accumulators, I think. When you make them initially, they accumulate very little electricity and do not return anything. You use all the current to make the accumulator, to tune it. The successive charges and discharges modify it until it manages to store electricity and return it normally. The same process will happen with the man we make."

"But if we force the load ..."

"It would take a thousand years. Look at the tuning process of our brain; It is millions of years old, the entire age of humanity. Our man would find himself, in intelligence—or perception, whatever you call it—in the same state as a newborn."

Donissoff, who had not taken his eyes off the glass, turned sharply to Sivel:

"This is all perfectly true, and while you were speaking, I was making the same considerations. But, however logical the reasoning is, it is only conjecture. I think this is precisely the flaw in your logic: we are created beings, not creators.

Who can say what faculties a nervous system will have, with the identical constitution to a man in full manhood? His very argument about electric batteries can support what I say: manufacturers, desperate for the time it takes to make lead sheets, cover the sheets with a layer of oxides, the same oxides that form naturally in batteries over time. That is to say: they give the newborn the nervous system of an adult. Why wouldn't our man be in the same condition, Sivel?"

"Maybe, but I don't think so."

At that moment, Donissoff got up and placed both fists on the table, staring at his associates. His attitude, which would have struck anyone else, was far from causing that impression in the case of Donissoff. On the contrary, the diamond temper of that soul rose to his limpid gaze. His angelic beauty took on a tone, not of hardness, but firmness, something, in short, of the sad beauty of a rebellious archangel.

"Listen to me," he said in a sharp, clear accent. "Let's make a man. The temptation is too great for us not to address it. But I have one condition, without which I do not commit to anything: you let me direct the tuning process, as Sivel says. I do not know yet what I will do, much less how: do you consent?"

"Yes, Donissoff, we agree!" Sivel and Ortiz answered at once, getting up.

The heat of a new triumph completely dissipated their weariness. The three scientists were once again ready to fight against the shadows of the unknown.

"One moment! Donissoff stopped them. Do you trust me?"

Then Sivel, who felt deep tenderness and adoration, put his hand on his shoulder:

"Sublime child!" He said, smiling, although unable to hide his emotion. Donissoff raised his beautiful head:

"Well! Let's see how the rat is doing."

In the middle of the laboratory, on the marble table, and focused by the bright light of the eight electric lamps with green shades, the rat was still lying on its back.

Ortiz was the first to lean over it, and after a moment of deep examination, he stood up pale:

"This animal is dying!" He said to Donissoff, looking into his eyes.

Donissoff and Sivel bent sharply over the rat and stared at the black beast, their eyes fixed on the heart of the animal, its dizzying beats making its skin vibrate with an electric-bellied rush.

The emotion of the three associates was too

great to allow them to speak. There, before their eyes, the rat was dying, returning to the nothing it had come from, taking with it the immense pride of its creators, the artificial rat.

Ten long minutes passed like this, until Donissoff's voice rang out, clear and icy, in that tragic silence:

"This animal has blood poisoning. Sivel, are you sure of its formulas?"

"The blood's formula, Donissoff?"

"Yes."

"Completely sure. In the test run, I overlooked the slightest dissociation of elements. I remember the rehearsal lasted two months."

"Still, do you want to bring your inventory?"

Ortiz had given the name "Inventory" to the notebook of formulas that governed the creation of the rat. They were all there, and when Sivel returned, Donissoff flipped through the notebook feverishly and paused at the equations of blood.

"Yes, that's fine; no, not that... " he murmured. "But that blood is poisoned nonetheless."

While Sivel and Ortiz analyzed the air expelled from the rat's lungs, Donissoff extracted a few drops of blood from the animal's veins and plunged into his analysis. For a long time in the laboratory, it was silent except for the knock of the glass tubes. At last, Donissoff spoke.

"Is something wrong there?"

"Nothing," Ortiz said. "The air is normal. And there?"

"Yes. The phosphate level is off the charts."

For months and months, the three associates had struggled in the formation of bone tissue. Despite the successful trial, they always feared that the phosphates were not well fixed. Later, new triumphs made them forget that concern. But now, everything was clear: the bones were dissolving; the phosphates, now in the bloodstream, were killing the rat.

Slowly the three men circled the animal again. Three years, one thousand ninety-five days of struggle as they had never had it, of energy as they had never found it, of passion as they had never felt, all those days of ardent hope crumbled in tragic silence, dragging pride with them, also in pieces, of those men of genius.

Minute after minute, the bones dissolved, poisoning the rat's blood. And when the rat was finally immobile at half-past nine at night, reinstated after two hours of prodigious life with the nothingness of which it had come out by dint of human genius, the three associates did not say a single word. Without looking at each other, without making a gesture, broken, overwhelmed with fatigue and intellectual fatigue, they lay down.

In the state of fatigue in which they were, sleep gave them up as soon as they laid their heads down. But late at night, possibly three in the morning, Donissoff's voice rang out:

"Two more carbon atomicities ...!"

"One would do, Donissoff!" Sivel's voice answered instantly. "But decreasing the ..."

"Nitrogen! Yes, there was too much!" Ortiz continued. The three associates, instead of sleeping, had spent the night working out the formula for the bone tissue.

They fell asleep right away. The formula was now perfect: the bones would not dissolve anymore.

And so, restarting the equations, analysis, and trials that were almost their reason for existing for three years, the three associates made a man. Element by element, milligram for milligram, everything had been neatly dosed, tested, and executed.

So in the early morning of June 11, 1909, when Donissoff gave his final plunger blow into the veins of the prodigious spawn, the associates' chests opened in a deep sigh, like a tremendous outpouring of hope that this time, he would survive.

And he was not frustrated. The same decoration that ten months ago had framed the vivification of the rat now presided over that of the beautiful created being. The laboratory in silence and dim light: the central table— again now with thick blankets—vividly illuminated by the eight green-screen lamps, the suffocating mist of the last time: the three associates surrounded the body in equal tension of spirit.

Donissoff, with his ear to the man's heart, looked like a statue while Sivel fixed his eyes on the thermometer inserted into the man's mouth. Ortiz pressed the man's feet between his hands, observing the temperature.

For two eternal minutes, none of them moved. At last, Donissoff sat up, brushing his blond hair from his forehead.

"That's it," he said. "Take the thermometer, Sivel. Same thing, Ortiz. Turn off the power. Twenty-five degrees is enough."

The associates put incredible perfection into every single detail. They had such mutual faith in the inventive genius of Donissoff, Sivel's scrutiny, and Ortiz's perseverance that the three associates did not even remotely feel the crazy enthusiasm of the other time when the rat lived.

Their souls vibrated with glory, no doubt, but

that glory was too high for it to manifest itself in physical turbulence. So they sat on the other table, their legs dangling, silently looking at their work.

The being that lay on his back in front of them was a man of medium height, of significant proportion. He was twenty-five years old. The features had a surprising serenity. The eyes were closed, and the chest rose and fell rhythmically.

Donissoff, Sivel, and Ortiz had done the impossible, going from that rat, which had devoured itself after two hours of existence, to that beautiful being that lay naked, breathing harmoniously.

It also had a name. Since from the first moments they got to work, they had felt the need to call their man-in-training somehow, Ortiz had proposed calling him Biogeno, that is: "I spawn life." In truth, they were the creature's creators, but they liked the name.

After a long time of silent contemplation of his work, Sivel raised his voice in that silence:

"We are done, Donissoff. Now it's up to you. If we wake him up, he will open his eyes and look, and if we put him down, he will remain standing where we left him. If Biogeno does walk, he will collide with everything because he has no notion of obstacles."

"You don't expect us to see that, do you? In that case, it would be better if we just shot ourselves."

Donissoff, staring at the table, seemed not to have heard. His expression had that stamp of the relentless will of decisive occasions.

"No! He finally answered. We have not done that to our disgrace. Do you remember the promise you made me when we decided to work on this ...? Sivel, Ortiz! I need to animate the creature."

"Understood, Donissoff! You don't need to tell us more."

"Yes, there's something I need to tell you ..."

"What, Donissoff?"

His face contorted, and a steel beam crossed his archangel gaze.

"One moment. Just give me one moment!"

And he left the laboratory.

Donissoff entered, accompanied by a poorly dressed man, very skinny and with a yellowish countenance. He wore dark glasses. The subject, evidently timid, looked in great surprise at the three men until his gaze fixed on the electric lamps, the glowing table, and the man lying on it.

"I told you," Donissoff said to him, "I chloroformed him. We need his help to complete this. Allow me a second!" And turning to Sivel and Ortiz, he said quickly in English:

"This man must be restrained at once. Let's not waste a minute."

So abrupt was the revelation for the two associates that despite their dominance over themselves, their eyes were wide open.

"Go! Do not forget your promises. Right away!" Donissoff repeated in his voice.

"Donissoff!" Ortiz murmured.

"Ortiz!" The one squeaked through his teeth, his gaze embracing him. And he turned to the man. The latter, eyes wide with stupor and mistrust, took a step back. But another put his hand on his shoulder:

"Ortiz ...! Sivel ...!" He called in his clear, cutting voice. And in a second, the associates restrained the man who was now tied and seated in a chair. His glasses fell during the struggle; he was livid, hair wild, and face pierced with terror.

The three panting associates did not bother to move away to speak.

"All well?" Asked Sivel and Ortiz', gazes fixed on Donissoff's.

"Very well!" He replied. "It is done."

"Speak in English, Donissoff," Sivel said. And he added, "What do you mean?"

"That man...?"

"Yes."

"What are we going to do to him ...?"

"We will torture him."

Sivel, who was about to add something, stopped and fixed his gaze deeply on Donissoff. He looked at him calmly but very pale.

"We will what?"

"We need an intense production of pain, an over-acute current of pain, to provoke in his nervous system a sensitivity that only the years would give. Remember the discussion we had at the beginning, comparing our work to an accumulator."

Ortiz explained everything several days later:

If someone winds an insulated wire around an iron cylinder and an electric current passes through the wire, the iron becomes magnetized. Suppose someone inserts the cylinder into the spool, over another perfectly insulated wire, without any communication with the cylinder. In that case, the electric current of the cylinder passes by influence to the spool, with greatly amplified energy. This phenomenon is known as a Rumkhorff spool.

This explanation was not necessary for Sivel and Ortiz. They saw immediately, with a shudder, where Donissoff was going.

Their faces reflected the admiration that bold stroke of genius or madness caused them. But to torture a man! Undoubtedly horrible; But for those three men who had sacrificed everything for this ideal, one his father's affection, another his love, another his fortune, the torment applied to an innocent being could not be an obstacle to the triumph of their scientific ideal. There was nothing more pure and simple than the hearts of those three men. For that reason, despite everything, their intelligence inexorably decided the necessary martyrdom. Their souls within there wept with compassion. In Donissoff, above all, he made the profound contrast between his archangel face and the terrible will that overcome his sufferings shudder as a dark battle flag thrust vigorously into his own heart. And for this very reason, the eyes of the poor captured man—livid with terror—widened when he saw Donissoff speaking, without realizing it, in French.

"Let's decide, Sivel! The more time we have, the better. Ortiz: open the stream a little."

"For torture ...?"

But he could not conclude. A scream of horror, a tearing cry had come from the poor man's throat as he heard the word "torture." Already infinitely afraid of the rope tying his wrists, that laboratory with its appearance of hell, and the three man-eating demons, his whole being had shattered into a scream when he saw what awaited him.

The wretch made a terrible effort to break the ropes and rolled on the floor with a convulsion. They lifted him, sat him down, and Donissoff, putting his hand on his arm, said coldly:

"It's useless for you to shout: absolutely no one can hear you from the street. Now, if the assurance that we suffer more than you with your pain can be of any use to you, have it."

The poor one, his eyes wide open and his face streaked with icy beads of sweat, stood motionless, following Donissoff with his eyes. From that moment on, he did not make a gesture, nor did he move, in a deep stupor.

Then they joined a table with the one on which Biogeno was lying and laid the victim naked. They held his wrists and feet to the table, and while Ortiz opened the current of his dynamo more to raise the temperature of the laboratory, Donissoff went to look for a small tool: pliers.

The immobilized man felt Donissoff's approach and the touch of his slender hand on one of his. For five seconds, the man's heart beat wildly, dying of anguished expectation. And suddenly, he screamed. One of his nails, caught by the edge with the pliers, had just been pulled off.

It was a single scream, but it carried with it a hysterical paroxysm of pain. The laboratory fell silent again. The three associates, pale as death and with their eyes fixed on Biogeno, had just noticed a slight shudder on his eyelids.

"Did you see that ..." Ortiz murmured.

Neither responded. Yes, the current passed; the newly created being, virginally pure of sensations, had just felt the first shock of pain brought to its culmination.

A moment later, another scream rang out, more heartbreaking than the first; another fingernail pulled off with the pliers had disappeared from the finger.

And with long intervals, the screams followed one another but lengthening more and more in a lamentable rattle.

The three associates, fixed their eyes on Biogeno, noted the growing tremor of his eyelids while his appearance of serenity began to face. He was acquiring that something tired, painful seriousness that characterizes the expression of the adult who has felt and suffered. The accumulator was charging.

But meanwhile, with each new scream, the pallor of the operators increased. Finally, when the torturer removed the sixth nail, Ortiz put his hand on Donissoff's arm and looked at him in deep anguish:

"I can't take it anymore, Donissoff ... I'm leaving."

Donissoff avoided his gaze and shook the waves from his hair without answering him.

"I'm suffering too much ..." Ortiz continued in a low voice.

"Me too," Donissoff said, his face white and drawn. "But I will go to the end."

Ortiz withdrew. Sivel slammed a still-retained operating clamp to the ground on the eighth scream and threw himself onto a table. Donissoff stared at him for a while and, going toward him, gently passed his hand over his head.

"Go away, Sivel!" I will continue alone.

Sivel lifted his disfigured face, whiter than marble, and fixed his eyes on Donissoff's. For long seconds those two men of formidable mettle observed each other. During those seconds, both returned to the past full of blood from their souls.

But this time, the screams broke the steel of Sivel's will. He couldn't resist anymore.

"Go away, Sivel," Donissoff repeated softly. Sivel

left and sunk with Ortiz on the dining room couches; they continued to hear the heartbreaking wails of the tortured.

Half an hour passed like this. Ortiz, with his hands clasped behind his neck, was staring at the ceiling. Sivel, also motionless, was smoking. But the cigarette lasted only a few minutes. And after lighting the tenth, the screaming stopped.

A moment later, Donissoff entered, pale as death.

"I'm dying of thirst!" He exclaimed hoarsely. "Do you want to make tea, Ortiz? I'm a little tired."

In turn, he dropped onto the couch next to Ortiz, throwing his head back, his eyes closed.

They did not say a word for a long time. The silence seemed much deeper now.

"Is it done?" Sivel asked him at last, without looking at him.

"Yes, but I don't know … I was dying of thirst."

"And that bastard?" Ortiz told him.

"One moment, Ortiz! Let me rest a moment …! He's passed out now."

When they finished their tea, they got up and went to the laboratory. On the brightly lit tables, the two bodies lay, side by side. The man now looked cadaverously thin, his belly was hideously hollow, and the protruding ribs, projected up in contrast, seemed to break through his skin. His face was pale, and his eyes sunk deep into their sockets. Two threads of blood fell from his nostrils, cutting parallel to his lips and getting lost in his beard. He did not have a single nail on his fingers.

The three associates leaned over Biogeno. Yes, that closed mouth had screamed; those eyes had seen, that forehead, no longer smooth, he had thought! The trembling of the eyelids stopped, but his expression was different: the face of a man who has lived, loved, suffered.

Despite the emotions of that day and the terrible shocks they had just suffered, the three experimenters felt their souls refreshed with glorious pride. Biogeno's heart worked with absolute precision, the lungs burned its oxygen down to the last atom, and the brain now lived. His nervous system was no longer that of a newborn: his brain had lived through an entire existence of sensations.

But to do so, in two hours, he had devoured everything that can be painful in a human organism.

The eyes of his creators finally turned away from him, settling on the victim.

"You've suffered horribly," Ortiz murmured,

lowering his lower eyelid. It was urgent to lift his depression; they peeled off the ligatures and carried him to Donissoff's bed with exquisite care. There, thanks to an injection of caffeine and lavished care on him, the wretch came to himself. Eyes wide with stupor slowly swept the room and finally fixed on the three faces watching him. Suddenly his face twisted horribly. He uttered a desperate cry against a new terror: he had just recognized Donissoff.

"Get back!" Sivel said in his ear. "Your presence would just drive him crazy."

Donissoff came out, and then Sivel and Ortiz had the arduous job of reassuring the tortured miserable, succeeding after a long half-hour. Then they left, locking the door behind.

The three associates finally found themselves alone.

"It's time for us to finish," Ortiz exclaimed, passing his hand over his forehead. "I have the feeling that we have lived a thousand years on this day."

"Yes, we are done!" Sivel observed.

"Why not? Look at that expression. That man has already forty years of cerebral life."

"Do you feel fear, Sivel?" Donissoff turned to him as he picked up his Pravatz syringe.

"I don't know ..." Sivel replied, shaking his head. "I fear a lot, at least ... But I fear something else."

"What?"

"I'm not sure ... Inject Biogeno, Donissoff."

Donissoff injected his serum into Biogeno's belly, and a moment later, he opened his eyes. It is easy to realize the deep anxiety the three experimenters observed that first tangible life manifestation. Biogeno's gaze, clear, limpid, but utterly devoid of expression, was fixed directly on the ceiling.

A minute passed like this, in profound silence. Donissoff, Sivel, and Ortiz watched that look, and that gaze fixed on the ceiling, without blinking. At last, there was a murmur.

"I don't know," Ortiz whispered.

Instantly, Biogeno's head turned to where the voice had sounded, and his eyes, with an expression of deep concern, looked at the three men. All three felt a deep shudder upon examining those eyes.

"Donissoff ...! That look!" Ortiz murmured.

"Yes," Donissoff said palely. "I know that look too."

"That's what ..." Sivel was going to add. But the

words cut off in his mouth.

Biogeno, with an expression of acute suffering, has just picked up his hands, touching his nails.

"That's what I was afraid of!" Sivel resumed, frowning. "He has absorbed all the tortures of the other! We have made a monster of pain, Donissoff!"

"No! He replied with his pale archangel face. The pain is still on the edge of the nerve. It won't last much longer."

Then a voice was heard that was not from any of the three experimenters.

"Oh! The ones!"

The first movement of Donissoff, Sivel, and Ortiz was to turn sharply toward the door of the room in which the poor tortured lay: they had heard his voice. It was his voice, yet the voice came from the table: it was he who was speaking from Biogeno's body.

All three men shook violently. That simple phrase already demonstrated sensation, perception, everything that makes the adult a superior being. But the look belonged to the other! The voice belonged to the other!

"We have done something terrible, Donissoff!" Sivel cried again, running his hand across his anguished forehead. "That man has no life of his own. It is a mannequin; we have transmitted the soul of the other."

Donissoff straightened, and as his gaze turned steely again, as in all cases in which an explosion of will or genius burst from his soul, he put his hand on Sivel's shoulder.

"I have never assured you in advance of a thing of which I was not entirely sure. That being has a life of its own or will have it, influenced by the soul of the wretch. But it will dissipate as soon as he wakes up. And then..."

"Then what, Donissoff?"

"Then," Donissoff continued a little slowly, looking elsewhere. "Then it is possible that Biogeno still suffers a lot. I feared ..."

But he could not conclude. Biogeno, who after that sentence of suffering had fallen into a deep slumber, had just opened his eyes and gave a hysterical cry.

"That's what I was afraid of!" Donissoff exclaimed, livid.

A new scream rang out, and Biogeno jumped to his feet. The three associates threw themselves on him, and as soon as Biogeno felt that contact on his body, he burst into screams of terrible pain.

"Donissoff!" Sivel exclaimed after a while of silence, getting up. "Donissoff!" he repeated, staring at him: "Let's kill him!"

Ortiz, who straddled the chair with his head resting on his arms crossed on the back, slowly raised his pale face. All you could hear was Biogeno's breathing.

"We have made a monster, Donissoff!" Sivel repeated hoarsely. "Let's kill him! Let's be merciful."

Donissoff, who had not made a single gesture so far, got up. He went to bed, pulsed those arteries, listened to those lungs, and turned at last with wet eyes.

"Comrades! You know with how much love and energy we have worked together for four years. I ask you for one day, nothing more than one day! If your nervous system is not appeased by this time tomorrow, we will destroy our work. But one day, please, Sivel!"

And sitting at the foot of the bed, he let his head fall back.

However, for Sivel and Ortiz, who knew Donissoff deeply, that exclamation was more fearsome than any profound protest of discouragement.

How solid and deep were the emotions to break their nerves! Without a doubt, the work was extraordinary, and they had contributed the intimate substance of their souls, transformed into talent and energy. But neither Sivel nor Ortiz were unaware of Donissoff's doing.

Ortiz wanted to go to Donissoff, but Sivel held him back with a gesture. They froze.

A moment later, Donissoff got up. There was not the slightest trace of discouragement. His forehead, his eyes, his entire expression had the usual clarity.

"I think we could go to bed," he said simply.

Sivel and Ortiz nodded very willingly. Before they closed the room's windows and doors hermetically to avoid stimulating Biogeno's senses as much as possible, they left. Sivel and Donissoff slept in the laboratory on a simple blanket.

The next day the three associates got up very early. They felt bruised, broken by the emotions of the last twenty-four hours in which they had seen the fulfillment, failure, and resurgence of their three-year dream. They went to the dining room, where they had breakfast with oranges since they weren't hungry. The acidic juice was a great pain reliever for their dry throats, and then, a little more comforted, they went to Sivel's room, where the tortured man, with both hands bandaged, was still sleeping.

He only woke up when the three experimenters

were at his side. His eyes widened in a deep black circle; dark circles of past suffering and terror wandered dully across the ceiling.

"Good morning," Sivel said, putting his hand on his head. "How are you?"

The wretch's gaze, which went heavily from one to the other, ended by fixing on Sivel's. And slowly, like an electric lamp that begins to light up little by little, he revived.

"I'm fine." He replied after a while, in a voice that emerged broken from the depths of his nature, still trembling.

"Much pain there?" Sivel continued.

"No ... nothing ... it doesn't hurt ..."

"How...! But take a good look: pain, right? So nothing hurts, nothing?"

The other closed his eyes, and his lips trembled for a while.

"No, nothing..."

Sivel and Ortiz looked at each other intensely. Donissoff, staring at the bandaged stumps, did not move a single muscle. Then Sivel came out, returning at once with a needle for sewing wounds. He leaned over him and, pressing hard on his wrist, asked:

"Feel this?"

"No."

Then Sivel plunged the entire needle into his forearm.

"Feel this?"

"No."

Sivel, pale, stood up. He covered the man again and, followed by his companions, left the room.

"The man is dying," he said when they were alone in the laboratory. Donissoff didn't respond in the first few moments.

"We have killed him. We destroyed his nerves. They are incapable of even the slightest sensitive reaction. Tomorrow he will not see, the day after, he will not hear, and then he will not breathe."

"We've drained the battery too much," Ortiz observed.

"And the accumulator, on the other hand, has been overcharged," Sivel supported, staring for a moment. When he lifted it, Donissoff was no longer there.

"And Doni ...?" I was going to ask. And a terrible scream, a true howl of pain, chilled his words. They jumped into his room, but Donissoff was closing the door on the outside at that moment.

"What, Donissoff? What happened?" Ortiz exclaimed.

"Nothing," he said. "I walked in, and he was in the middle of the room."

"And that scream?"

"He screamed as soon as he saw the light."

Another cry of pain, indeed, had just been heard. It was Biogeno, whose vibrating nervous system elicited screams of acute pain. A small beam of light gave him the effect of a dazzling glow in the middle of the pupil. If he touched an object, he received a violent burn. And taste, hearing, smell, all the organs of sensation, put to a degree of terrible excitability by their creators, kept that wretch in the middle of the room, trembling, anguished, drenched in the cold sweat of torment.

Yes! He had stolen, absorbing every last vibration, all the nervous power that arises from a tortured person. The absorption had been complete, decisive, and fatal: while one felt too much until howling in pain at the impression of a slight ray of light, the other, with his nerves drained and dead, was going to lose his life because he felt nothing.

The three men had frozen before the closed door. The second scream had followed a third, and then silence again.

"Who knows!" Sivel murmured. "Maybe he'll lose that sensitivity soon. Let's go back in, Donissoff."

As soon as they turned the key, an anguished cry proved to them that the slight noise of the key had tortured his eardrum. They backed away, their hopes shattered, while the screaming in the room continued: this time of much more intensity and duration than the first time.

The creaking of a door, the light coming through it, was no longer necessary: the muffled noises from the street, the almost invisible leaks of light, the mere contact of the feet on the ground were for that nature that had come to life through of screams of pain an inexhaustible source of torments. The experimenters had not intended to subject him to the torture of feeding for an instant. Apart from the irresistible pain that a simple drink of water would have caused Biogeno, it would have been necessary to put their hands on him, thus exposing him to great suffering.

The other, meanwhile, the miserable tortured, was dying out in the total emptiness of his body. He no longer saw, heard, or felt anything. He lay on his back, motionless, dead alive. His heart beat more and more weakly. His breathing trailed off, and that young body, full of life two days before, was hardly a plant organism, an insensitive machine that had emptied every last drop in explosive charges of pain.

And in Donissoff's room, the screams of torture continued, high-pitched, ongoing, until, at the end of the third day, they suddenly ceased. The three associates entered and found Biogeno passed out on the ground. They laid him down and stood by his side, deep in tumultuous musings.

For two days, they had not seen him; they had not seen that human being thought, planned, and executed by them. And how many lost hopes! What a disaster and what a triumph, with those nerves that bled alive from excess sensation! But that was not what they had intended. So there he was, passed out from nervous exhaustion, at last, after two days of torture. But he would come to himself soon.

"What do you think, Donissoff?" Sivel asked. "A thick injection of morphine? It might work."

"Yes," Donissoff said, his voice lost. "It would hold up well, but we would kill the soul. And what we need is to reduce the external sensitivity, nothing more. Then, maybe we can do something else."

"What?"

"Unload the accumulator."

"It's what has been happening since the day before yesterday."

"Yes, but short-circuited."

Sivel stared at him intently, and his distorted face paled.

"I don't want any more torture, Donissoff!" He said hoarsely.

"We won't torture anyone, Sivel," he objected. "But we could hypnotize someone. In this state, it is easy to receive the excess load of Biogeno."

"But to whom?"

"To me."

Sivel and Ortiz turned sharply to Donissoff. His archangel beauty sparkled under the influence of his genius and his will. Sivel, who had lowered his gaze on Biogeno again, raised it this time completely contracted:

"Donissoff! For the love of this world, don't do that!"

"For God's sake ..." Donissoff murmured, a bitter smile playing on his lips. And his gaze lost in the void reconstructed another scene of the secret committee, there, far away, in which he had sacrificed more than his own life.

"It is necessary! Back in Russia, I did some hypnotism experiments. We all needed to keep our active and passive power of suggestions. As you understand, it will be easy for me to transform myself into an accumulator in this state. It will be necessary to torture Biogeno."

"No, no, Donissoff!" Ortiz exclaimed. "I don't want to hear another single cry of torture!"

"Neither do I; that's why I want to change this unsustainable state of affairs. We added into this miserable machine of suffering everything that still unites us with life. The pains you may feel are nothing compared to the continuous torture of this poor being. Besides, Sivel, two or three shakes are enough. My nerves will pick up the current to return it as soon as the hypnotic state ceases. Look at this."

And it was obvious: the problem thus found a prodigious and elementary solution. Sivel and Ortiz's chest opened to a new wave of hope, which this time would lead them to triumph.

Then, alive, feverishly, they arranged everything. The associates transported Biogeno to the laboratory and laid him tightly bound on the table where he was born into his miserable life. Donissoff stretched out beside him, pressing heavily on Biogeno's hand. The torture room looked the same as the first time: the dark laboratory in the corners, the marble tables vividly illuminated by the electric lamps with green shades, the mute experimenters, and the quiet atmosphere of the room that seemed to wait in anguish for new cries of torture.

Sivel leaned over Donissoff and fixed his gaze deeply on Donissoff's eyes. Ortiz, motionless, pulsed Biogeno. There was not the slightest noise in the laboratory.

After a while, Donissoff's eyes closed. Sivel placed the thumb and forefinger of his hand on his eyelids, gently squeezing his eyes.

"Are you asleep, Donissoff?"

"Not yet."

A long time passed. The two men heard the buzzing of a fly throughout the laboratory.

"Asleep, Donissoff?"

This time the answer was delayed.

"Yes, I am asleep."

Sivel then turned to Ortiz.

"Ready?" He asked in a low voice.

"He's already starting to shudder ... let's get started right away!"

There was no time to lose. Sivel leaned over Donissoff again.

"Donissoff!" He said in a slow voice to insinuate the suggestion more firmly. "You have a great nervous weakness and need strong arousal ... Can you hear me?"

"Yes."

"When the impression you feel becomes painful, okay? When you feel pain, you will wake up immediately."

"Yes."

"Do you hardly feel pain, Donissoff?"

"Yes," Sivel replied, calm. With this peremptory suggestion, there was nothing to fear; the slightest disturbance would be impossible.

What happened then was so terrible that neither Sivel nor Ortiz have since been able to reconsider just how long it took for the awful catastrophe to take place. Sivel barely finished straightening up when Biogeno stirred violently. It was necessary at all costs to prevent him from waking up.

"Quick, Ortiz!" Sivel exclaimed. "Torture him!"

Ortiz bent over the wretch with his instrument of horror, and a second later, a horrible, superhuman scream, such as had never been heard, a true expression of pain brought to its paroxysm echoed through the gloomy laboratory. And behind him, another cry, but hoarse, with an exploding heart, drove the operators crazy.

Donissoff had just straightened up violently, his

eyes bulging and his mouth hideously open.

"Donissoff!" Ortiz and Sivel yelled at the same time, rushing over him. But Donissoff had fallen backward again, with a hoarse sigh, dead, shattered by that abominable pain machine that he had created with his genius and that had just unloaded all his accumulated suffering, killing Donissoff.

Ortiz and Sivel, speechless with horror, were stunned. Their companion, the greatest and noblest of all men, that creature of genius and sacrifice, struck down forever! And lost forever! He was there dead, that archangel of genius who had created the most significant thing that is possible to develop in this world!

Sivel, with a deep, hoarse sob, fell on the hero's chest.

"Donissoff, dear boy!" He exclaimed. "What have we done to you?"

Ortiz didn't have the strength to wipe away the thick tears that were rolling down his cheeks.

They would never aspire to anything again! Their entire future was already over, as Donissoff was dead.

THE VAMPIRE

These are the last lines I write. A moment ago, I noticed the doctors taking significant glances at me: the extreme nervous depression in which I lie comes to an end. I have suffered for a month from a strong shock followed by brain fever. Still poorly recovered, I suffer a relapse that leads me directly to the sanatorium.

The nervous war patients have called these isolated establishments "living tombs," where one lies motionless in the gloom, preserved by all possible means from the slightest noise. If someone fired a gun in the outer corridor, the noise alone would kill half the sick. The ongoing explosions of grenades have made these soldiers what they are.

They lie sprawled across their beds, stunned, inert, genuinely dead in the silence that shrouds their undone nervous system like thick cotton. But the slightest sudden noise, the closing of a door, the rolling of a spoon, triggers a horrible scream from them.

Such is their nervous system. Once, these

men were spirited and feared soldiers. Today, the abrupt fall of a plate would kill at least one of them. Although I have not been in the war, I could not resist an unexpected stimulus either. A mere sunray from the corner of a window would make me scream. However, living in the shadows does not alleviate my ills.

In the sepulchral gloom and eternal silence of the vast room, I lie motionless, eyes closed, dead. But inside me, my whole being is lurking. My entire being and agony are a white and exhausted longing until death, which must come shortly. Moment after moment, I hope to hear beyond the silence, crumbled and dotted in the dizzying distance, a slight crackle. In the darkness of my eyes, I hope every moment to see, white, concentrated, and tiny, the ghost of a woman.

In a recent and immemorial past, that ghost walked through the dining room, stopped, resumed her path without knowing where she was going. Back then, I was a robust man with good humor and healthy nerves.

One day I received a letter from a stranger asking for information about a publication I made about the N1 rays.

Although it is not uncommon to receive demands like that, he drew my attention by his interest in a short, obscure article I published long ago. I barely remembered the article in question. I answered him, however, giving him the approximate date of its publication with the newspaper's name in which the article appeared. Afterward, I completely forgot about the incident.

A month later, I received another letter from the same person. He wondered if the experiment I mentioned in my article was just a fantasy of my mind or was real. I was somewhat intrigued by the persistence of the stranger who was asking me, a lazy amateur of science, the results I obtained from the profound studies on the matter. And despite this, which my cultured correspondent could not ignore, he insisted on verifying, through my mouth, the integrity and precision of certain optical phenomena that any man of science could confirm for him.

I hardly remembered, as I said, what I had written about the rays in question. With great effort, I found the information the individual requested at the bottom of my memory. I answered him that if he was referring to the phenomenon by which sunny bricks lose the ability to emit N1 rays, I could guarantee that it was accurate. Gustave Le Bon, among others, had verified the phenomenon. So, I answered and once again forgot about the N1 rays.

However, I only forgot about the rays for a brief time. A third letter arrived, acknowledging my report, with the following final lines:

"This is not how I want to get a personal impression of you. But since I understand that continuing our correspondence in this fashion might come to annoy you, I beg you to allow me a few moments of conversation at your house or wherever you would like."

Of course, I had already dismissed the initial idea of dealing with a madman. Even then, I think, I suspected what he expected of me, why he was interested in my knowledge, and where the mysterious correspondent wanted to go. I was sure it was not my poor scientific knowledge that interested him.

And I finally saw this, as clear as a man sees his image in the mirror, observing him, when the next day Don Guillen de Orzúa y Rosales—that's what he called himself—sat opposite me at the desk, and began to talk. First of all, I will describe his physique. He was a middle-aged man whose figure and measure of words denounced the man of long and intelligently enjoyed fortune. The first thing one would notice about him is his habit of riches.

The warm tone of his skin around his eyes was striking, like that of people who study cathode rays. He combed his black hair with an exact part to the side, and his calm and almost cold gaze expressed the same self-assurance and the same measure of his relaxed gesture. The first words we exchanged were the following:

"Are you Spanish?" I asked him, surprised by the lack of a peninsular accent in a man with such a surname.

"No," he answered briefly, and after a short pause, he explained the reason for his visit. Without being a man of science"—he said, crossing his hands on the table—"I have had some experiences on the phenomena I have alluded to in my correspondence. My fortune affords me the luxury of a laboratory far superior, unfortunately, to my ability to use it. I have not discovered any new phenomenon. I know something about the singular physiology of the N1 rays, and I would not have insisted on them again if the recommendation of your article by a friend, first, and the article itself, later, had not aroused my badly asleep curiosity about the N1 rays. You suggest the parallelism between certain auditory waves and visual emanations. If I have made myself understood well, I beg you to answer this question: Did you know of any experiment in this matter when you wrote your article, or was the suggestion of these embodiments only imaginative speculation? The N1 rays are the reason, Mr. Grant, that has led me to write to you twice, and then they have brought me to your house, perhaps to make you uncomfortable.

With that said, and with his hands always folded, he waited.

I responded immediately. But with the same

speed that a long memory is analyzed and crumbled before answering, I remembered the suggestion to which the visitor had alluded: if the retina impressed by the intense contemplation of a portrait can influence a sensitive plate to the point of obtaining a "double" of that portrait, in the same way, the living forces of the soul can, under the excitement of such emotional rays, not produce, but rather "create" an image in a visual and tangible circuit. Such was the thesis supported in my article.

"I'm not sure," I answered immediately, "that there have been any such experiments... There has been nothing more than imaginative speculation, as you very well say. There is nothing serious in my thesis."

"So you don't believe in your thesis?"

And with always calm folded hands, my visitor looked at me.

That look—which I noticed for the first time—was what had pre-enlightened me about the genuine reasons my visitor had for knowing more about my thesis.

But I didn't answer.

"It is neither a mystery to you nor me," he continued, "that the N1 rays alone will never be able to impress anything other than bricks or sunny portraits. Another aspect of the problem is the one that brings me to distract you from your precious moments."

"You asked me a question, so will you grant me an answer?" I interrupted, smiling. "Perfect! And you, Mr. Rosales, do you believe in the thesis?"

"You know that I do." He replied.

If between the gaze of a stranger who throws his cards on the table and that of another who hides his, there has ever been the certainty that both of them had the same hand—under those circumstances, we found ourselves.

There is only one exciting force capable of launching a soul into an explosion: this force is the imagination. My visitor was not interested in the N1 rays at all. s

"So do you believe," I said, "in infra-photographic prints? Do you suppose I'm the subject?"

"I'm sure," he replied.

"Have you tried it on yourself?"

"Not yet, but I will try. Being sure that you could not have had that urge is why I have come to see you."

"But suggestions and ideas abound," I began to observe. "The madhouses are full of them."

"No. The mental institutions are full of abnormal occurrences, but not ordinary ideas, like yours. Everything that one can conceive is within the realm of possibility, or so they say. There is a straightforward way of telling the truth by which nobody could doubt its veracity. You have that gift."

"My imagination is a bit sick ..." I argued, beating back.

"Mine is sick too," he smiled. "But it's time—he added, getting up—not to distract you more. I will specify the end of my visit in brief words: Do you want to go over your thesis with me? Do you feel strong enough to take the risk?"

"Of a failure?" I asked.

"No. It is not failure what we should fear."

"Then what?"

"The contrary."

"I think the same," I agreed after a pause. "Are you sure, Mr. Rosales, of your nervous system?"

"Very," he began to smile with his usual calm. "It would be my pleasure to see you again. Will you allow me to meet another day again? I live alone, I have few friends, and my knowledge of you is too rich not to want to count you among them."

"I would be delighted, Mr. Rosales," I replied.

And an instant later, the strange man left my company. Extraordinary, no doubt. An educated man, of great fortune, without a country or friends, had everything on his side to excite my curiosity. He could be a maniac, but what is undoubted is that he possessed great willpower. And for the beings that live on the border of the rational beyond, the will is the only sesame that can open the doors of the eternally forbidden.

To shut yourself up in the darkness with a sensitive projection before your eyes and contemplate it until you imprint on it the features of a loved woman is not an experience that costs your life. Rosales could try it, do it, without any genius set free coming to claim his soul. But the inescapable and fatal slope to which those fantasies can drag someone was what disturbed me.

Despite his promises, I didn't hear from Rosales for some time. One afternoon, chance put us side by side in the central passage of a movie theater when we were both leaving. Rosales withdrew slowly, his head held high in the rays of light and shadows from the projected lantern.

He seemed distracted by it, as I had to call him twice for him to hear me.

"You give me great pleasure," he said. "Do you have any spare time, Mr. Grant?"

"Not much," I replied.

"Perfect. Just ten minutes. Let's go somewhere."

When we were in front of two cups of coffee that were steaming precipitously, we exchanged the following words:

"What's new, Mr. Rosales?" I asked. "Have you made any progress?"

"Nothing, if you mean something other than a small impression. I will not continue repeating any such experiments anymore, either. There may be more interesting things near us. When you saw me a moment ago, I was following the beam of light that crossed the room. Are you interested in the cinema, Mr. Grant?"

"Very much."

"I was sure. Do you think that those projection rays agitated by the life of a man carry nothing to the screen but an icy electrical magnification? And forgive my poor choice of words. I have not slept for days; I have almost lost the ability to sleep. I drink coffee all night, but I don't sleep. Mr. Grant: Do you know what life is like in a painting, and how one bad painting differs from a good one? The oval portrait of Poe lived because the artist imbued it with "life itself." Do you think that a simple photographic illusion is capable of deceiving in this way the deep sense that a man possesses of reality?"

And he was silent, waiting for my answer.

Most people ask questions without reason, but when Rosales did it, he didn't do it in vain. He was seriously asking for an answer.

But what to answer to a man who asked me that question with the usual measured and polite voice? After a moment, however, I replied:

"I think you are half right. There is, without a doubt, something more than galvanic light in a film, but it is not life. There are also spectra."

"I have never heard," he objected, "that a thousand motionless men in the dark have desired a specter."

There was a long pause, which I broke by getting up.

"It's ten minutes now, Mr. Rosales," I smiled.

He did the same.

"You have been very kind to listen to me, Mr. Grant. Would you like to take your kindness to accept an invitation to eat in my company next Tuesday? We will have dinner at my place. I had an excellent cook, but he is ill. But unless you are very demanding, which I don't expect, we will muddle through, Mr. Grant."

"Yes, for sure. I'd be delighted."

"Until then, Mr. Grant."

I had the impression that the invitation to eat had not been merely occasional, nor was the cook absent due to illness, nor would I find any of his service people in his house. I was wrong, however, because when I knocked, the butler greeted me. I was led by four servants, one after the other until I reached the anteroom, where after a long wait, a servant apologized for the absence of my host: he was ill. Although he had tried to get up to apologize, it had been impossible for him to do so. The gentleman would come to see me as soon as he could get up.

Behind the hieratic maid and under the ajar door, the bedroom carpet was brightly lit. I could hear nothing in the house.

The next day I received the following notice from Rosales:

"Fate, my friend, deprived me of the pleasure of your visit when you honored my home yesterday. Do you remember what I told you about my cook? Well, this time, I was the sick one. Don't be apprehensive: I'm okay today, and I'll be the same next Tuesday. Will you come? I owe you reparation."

I had once been wrong about my new friend. There was too much reluctance, silence, and smell of crime in his persona and realm for someone to take him seriously. No matter how confident Rosales was of his mental fortitude, it was evident to me that he had already begun to stumble over the parapet of madness.

In addition to my misgivings in associating myself with a man who, without being Spanish, insisted on using noble turns of language, I headed the following Tuesday to the palace of the former patient, more willing to amuse myself with what I heard than to enjoy the equivocation my host's dinner.

But dinner did exist, though not servants because the same porter led me through the house to the dining room.

An instant later, the house owner would open the door ajar, and when he recognized me, he would let me pass with a calm smile.

The first thing that caught my attention when I entered was the accentuation of the warm tone, like tanned by the sun or ultraviolet rays, that habitually colored my friend's cheeks and temples. He was wearing a tuxedo. The second thing I noticed was the size of the luxurious dining room, so large that the table, still placed in the front third of the room, seemed to be at the back of it. The table, covered with delicacies, had only three seats. Near the head of the background, I saw in a soirée dress a woman's silhouette.

So I wasn't the only guest. We walked through

the dining room, and the strong impression that that feminine silhouette had awakened in me from the first moment turned into an over-acute tension when I could clearly distinguish her. She was not a woman; she was a ghost, the smiling, low-cut, translucent specter of a woman.

After a brief moment, I stopped; but there was such an act in Rosales's attitude of being faced with the ordinary that I advanced beside him.

"I think you already know Mr. William Grant, ma'am," he said to the lady, who smiled in my honor, and Rosales to me.

"Perfectly," I replied, bowing pale as a dead man.

"So take a seat," said the owner of the house, "and deign to eat whatever you like the most."

Under any other circumstance, the fine rain of terror would have bristled and soaked me to the bone. But this time, I slipped into the vague stupor that seemed to float over everything.

"And you, ma'am, aren't you hungry?" I turned to the lady, noticing her empty plate.

"Oh no, sir!"—She answered with the tone of someone who apologizes for not having an appetite, and clasping her hands under her cheek, she smiled thoughtfully.

"Do you always go to the movie theater, Mr.

Grant?" Rosales asked me.

"Very often," I replied.

"I recognized you at once," the lady turned to me. "I've seen you many times..."

"Very few of your films have made it to us," I replied.

"But you've seen them all, Mr. Grant," smiled the owner of the house.

"Indeed," I agreed, and after an extremely long pause: "Are the faces visible from the screen?"

"Perfectly," she replied, and she added, a little surprised, "why wouldn't they?"

"Indeed..." I began to repeat, but this time within myself.

If I thought I was sure that I had not died in the street when I was heading to Rosales', I must ideally admit the trivial and mundane reality of the woman who was sitting with us.

The minutes passed as we chatted about light topics. As the lady brought her hands to her eyes for the third time, the owner of the house said: "Are you tired, ma'am? Would you like to lie down for a moment? Mr. Grant and I will try to fill up the time you leave empty by smoking."

"Yes, I'm a little tired ..." she agreed, getting

up. "With your permission," she added, smiling at both of them one after the other.

And she withdrew, carrying her rich suit de soirée along with the cabinets.

Rosales and I were left alone, in silence.

"What is your opinion about this?" He asked me after a while.

"I think," I replied, "that if I've misjudged you twice lately, I've gotten my first impression of you right."

"You've judged me crazy twice, haven't you?"

"It is not difficult to guess."

We remained silent for another moment. There was not the slightest alteration in Rosales's usual courtesy and even less in the reserve and restraint that distinguished him.

"You have terrible willpower ..." I murmured.

"Yes," he smiled. "How to hide it? I was sure of my observation when you found me in the cinema. It was "her," precisely. A large amount of life betrayed in his expression had revealed the possibility of the phenomenon to me. A motionless film is the impression of a moment of life, and this is known to everyone. But from the moment the tape begins to run under the excitement of light, voltage, and N1 rays, all of it is transformed into a vibrant trace of life, more alive than the fugitive reality and the most vivid memories that guide our life to death. But this only you and I know."

"I must confess to you," Rosales continued with a slightly slow voice, "that at first, I had some difficulties. By a deviation of the imagination, possibly, I embodied something without a name ... One of those things that must remain forever on the other side of the grave. It came to me and did not leave me for three days. The only thing it couldn't do was climb into bed. When you got home a week ago, I hadn't seen that being for two hours, so I gave the order to bring you in. But when its footsteps sounded, I saw it tense on the edge of the bed, trying to climb. No, it is not something we know in this World. It was a delusion of the imagination. It will not come back again. The next day I played with my life by ripping our guest out of the movie, and I saved her. If you decide to embody the equivocal life on the screen one day, be careful, Mr. Grant. Beyond and behind this very moment, there is Death. Let go of your imagination, stir it to the bottom, but keep it at all costs in the same direction well held, without allowing it to deviate. May I have a vulgar simile? In a hunting weapon, the imagination is the projectile, and the will is the sight. Aim right, Mr. Grant! And now, we will see our friend. She must have already recovered from her fatigue. Let me guide you."

The thick drapery that the lady transposed

opened onto a sitting room, vast in proportion to the dining room. At the back of this room, one could find a beautiful alcove, ascended by three steps. There was a couch in the middle, almost a bed because of its width. On the divan, under the light of numerous candles, rested the specter of a beautiful woman.

Although our footsteps did not sound on the carpet, she felt our presence as we ascended the steps. And she turned her head to us, with a smile still full of softness:

"I fell asleep," she said. "Forgive me, Mr. Grant, and you too, Mr. Rosales. This calm is so sweet."

"Don't sit up, ma'am, I beg you!"—Exclaimed the owner of the house, noticing her decision. "Mr. Grant and I will bring two chairs closer, and we can talk calmly."

"Oh, thanks! I'm so comfortable like this." She murmured.

"Now, ma'am," he continued, "you can pass the time carelessly. Nothing urges us, and nothing worries our hours. Don't you think so, Mr. Grant?"

"Certainly," I agreed, with the same unawareness of time and the same amazement with which someone could announce that I had died fourteen years ago.

"I feel very well like this," replied the specter,

with both hands placed under her temple.

And we should have talked, I suppose, about pleasant and lively topics, because when I left, and the door closed behind me, the sun had been lighting the streets for long hours.

I got home and bathed right away to go out, but as I sat on the bed, I fell asleep, collapsed, and slept for twelve continuous hours. I retook a shower and left. My last memories floated, hovered traveling, without memory of place or time. I could have fixed them and faced each one, but all I wanted was to eat in a cheerful, noisy, and luxurious restaurant because I dreaded moderation, silence, and analysis. I was heading to a restaurant. And, instead, the door that I knocked on was the one to Rosales' house.

For a straight month, I have faithfully gone to dinner there, without my will having intervened at all. In the daylight hours, I am sure that an individual named William Grant has actively pursued the usual course of his life, with his routine chores and mishaps. After 9 pm, every night, I have found myself in the Rosales palace, in the dining room without service, first, and in the restroom, later.

As the dreamer of Armageddon, my life has been a hallucination, and I have been a ghost created to play that role. My actual existence has slipped away, contained as in a crypt, under the loving bedroom and the canopy of livid lamps.

"I wouldn't be entirely honest with you...." Rosales broke one night when our friend, legs and arms crossed, was thinking in silence. "It would not be sincere if I were to show my immense satisfaction with my work. I have taken severe risks to unite this pure and faithful companion to my destiny, and I would give the remainder of my years to give her a single moment of life. Mr. Grant, I have committed a crime without excuse. Do you think so?"

"I believe it," I replied. All his pains would not be enough to redeem a single wandering moan from that young woman.

"I know perfectly. And I have no right to support what I did."

"Undo it."

Rosales shook his head:

"No, nothing would remedy ..."

He paused. Then he looked up with the same calm expression and tone of voice that seemed to take him a thousand leagues away from the subject.

"I don't want any reluctance from you," he said. "Our friend will never emerge from the sorrowful fog in which she crawls unless there is a miracle. Only a tap of fate can grant her the life to which all creation is entitled if she is not a monster."

"What tap?" I asked.

"Her death. Back in Hollywood."

Rosales finished his cup of coffee as I sugared my own. Sixty seconds passed. I broke the silence:

"That wouldn't make any difference," I murmured.

"Why do you think that?" Rosales said.

"I'm sure ... I couldn't tell you why, but I know it. Also, it's impossible to do that."

"I am capable, Mr. Grant. For me, for you, this spectral creation is superior to any living spawn by the mere routine force of subsistence. Our companion is the work of conscience, do you hear, Mr. Grant? She responds to an almost divine purpose, and if I frustrate her, she will be my condemnation before the tumultuous divinities where no pagan god fits. Will you come from time to time during my absence? My servants set the table at nightfall, you know, and from that moment, everyone leaves the house except the doorman. Will you come?"

"I'll come," I said.

"It's more than I could hope for," Rosales concluded, bowing. I went there. If some night I was there at the appointed time for dinner, most of the time I was late, but always at the same time, with the punctuality of a man who is visiting his girlfriend's house. The young woman and I, at the table, used to talk animatedly on various topics. Still, in the living room, we hardly exchanged a word or two, and we fell silent immediately, won over by the stupor that flowed from the luminous cornices, which, finding the doors open or filtering through the locked eyes, impregnated the mansion with a gloomy silence.

As the nights went by, our brief phrases came to be materialized in monotonous observations and always on the same topic, which we did suddenly:

"He must be in Guayaquil by now," I said in a distracted voice.

Or she, many nights later:

"He's already left San Diego," she was saying at dawn.

One night, while I, with the cigar hanging from my hand, was making efforts to tear my gaze from the void, and she was wandering speechless with her cheek in her hand, she stopped suddenly and said:

"He's in Santa Monica."

She wandered for a moment still, and always with her face resting on her hand, she climbed the steps and stretched out on the couch. I felt her without moving my eyes from her because the room walls gave way, taking my eyesight; they fled with extreme speed in lines that converged without ever meeting.

"Santa Monica!" I thought, astonished.

How much time passed, I can't remember. Suddenly she raised her voice from the divan:

"He's home," she said.

With the last effort of volition that remained in me, I tore my gaze from her. Like a dead woman, the young woman lay motionless under the diamond-shaped ceilings embedded in the bedroom roof.

I closed my eyes and then saw a man raising a dagger over a sleeping woman in a sudden vision.

"Rosales!" I murmured, terrified; with a new flash of sparkle, the murderous dagger sank.

I do not remember anything else. I managed to hear a horrible scream—
possibly mine—and lost consciousness. When I came to my senses, I found myself at home, in bed. I had been unconscious for three days, suffering from a brain fever that lasted for more than a month. Little by little, I regained my strength. Someone told me that a man had taken me home late at night, passed out.

I remembered nothing, nor did I want to remember. I was highly lax in thinking about anything. Later I took short walks around the house, looking around with astonished eyes. I finally went out into the street, where I took a few steps without awareness of what I was doing, without memories, without purpose. When I saw a man approaching me in a silent room whose face was familiar to me, the memory and the lost consciousness abruptly heated my blood.

"I finally see you, Mr. Grant," Rosales told me, shaking my hand effusively. "I have followed the course of your illness with great concern since my return and did not doubt for a moment that you would be fine."

Rosales had lost weight. He spoke in a low voice as if he was afraid to be overheard. Over his shoulder, I saw the lighted bedroom and the well-known divan, surrounded, like a coffin, with high cushions.

"Is she there?" I asked.

Rosales followed my gaze and then returned his eyes to me calmly,

"Yes," he replied. And after a brief pause, "Come on," he told me.

We climbed the steps, and I leaned over the cushions. There was only one skeleton there. I felt Rosales's hand firmly clasping my arm.

"It's her, Mr. Grant." I do not feel any weight on my conscience, nor do I believe I have made a mistake. When I got back from my trip, she was gone. Mr. Grant. Do you remember seeing her the moment you lost consciousness?

"I don't remember ..." I murmured.

"It's what I thought. When I did what I did the night of her fainting, she disappeared from here. When I returned, I tortured my imagination to get her from The Beyond, which I have obtained! As long as she belonged to this World, I was able to embody her spectral life into a sweet creature. I took the life of the other to animate her ghost, and she, by all substantiation, puts her skeleton in my hands ..."

Rosales stopped. Again I had noticed his blank expression as he spoke.

"Rosales ..." I began.

"Pst! Please do not raise your voice. She is there." He interrupted me, lowering his tone even more.

"She...?"

"There, in the dining room ... Oh, haven't you seen her ...! But since I came back, she wanders from one place to another ... And I feel the touch of her dress. Pay attention for a moment. Can you hear her?"

In the silent mansion, through the atmosphere and the motionless lights, I heard nothing. We spent a while in complete silence.

"It's her," Rosales murmured, satisfied. "Hey now: dodge the chairs while walking ..."

For the space of a whole month, every night, Rosales and I have veiled the spectrum in bones and white lime of what was one day our stately guest. Behind the thick drapery that opens into the dining room, the lights are on. We know that she wanders there, stunned and invisible, in pain. When Rosales and I go to have coffee in the wee hours, perhaps she has already been occupying her seat for hours, she fixes her invisible gaze on us.

The nights follow each other, all the same. Under the atmosphere of amazement, time itself seems to stop. There has always been and will always be a skeleton under the ceiling, two friends in tuxedos in the living room, and a hallucination confined between the dining room chairs.

One night I found that the atmosphere changed. My friend's excitement was visible.

"I've finally found what I'm looking for, Mr. Grant," he said. "I already mentioned once that I was sure that you had not made any mistakes. Do you remember? Well then: I know now that I have committed it. You praised my imagination, no sharper than yours, and my will, which is far superior to yours. With these two forces, I created a visible creature, which we have lost, and a specter of bones, which will persist until who knows when. Do you know, Mr. Grant, what has been lacking in my work?"

"A purpose," I murmured, "that you thought was divine ..."

"You said so." I started from the enthusiasm of a dark room for a moving hallucination. I saw something more than a deception in the deep pulse of passion that stirs men before a vast and icy photograph. There must be more life there than a beam of lights and a metallic curtain. You've already seen it.

But I created sterilely, and this is the mistake I made. Love is not necessary for life, but it is essential to knock at the doors of death. If out of love I had killed, my child would throb with life on the couch today. I killed to create, without love, and I got life at its brutal root: a skeleton. Mr. Grant: Would you like to leave me for three days and come back next Tuesday to dine with us?

"With her...?"

"Yes, you, her and me ... Don't hesitate ... Next Tuesday."

When I opened the door myself, I saw her again, indeed, dressed in her usual magnificence, and I confess that I was delighted to notice that she, too, hoped to see me. She held out her hand, with the wide smile with which she considers a faithful friend again when she returns from a long journey.

"We have missed you very much, ma'am," I said effusively.

"I have missed you too, Mr. Grant! She replied, resting her face on both of her hands."

"Did you miss me? Really?"

"You? Oh yes, a lot!" And she smiled at me again for a long time.

At that moment, I realized that the house owner had not raised his eyes from his fork since we began to speak. Would it be possible ...?

"And our host, madam, didn't you miss him?"

"Him?" She murmured slowly, and slowly sliding his hand from her cheek, she turned her face to Rosales.

Then I saw through her eyes fixed on him the most insane flame of passion that any man has ever felt a woman. Rosales was looking at her too. And before that vertigo of feminine love expressed without reservation, the man paled.

"Him too ..." the young woman murmured in a quiet, exhausted voice.

Throughout the meal, she did not even notice

the home owner's presence while she chatted with me and did not for a moment abandon her game with the fork. But the two or three times their gazes met carelessly; I saw lightning in her eyes, and faint at once, the irrepressible heat of desire.

And she was a specter.

"Rosales!" I exclaimed as soon as we were alone for a moment. "If you keep a remnant of love for life, destroy her! She will kill you!"

"Destroy her? Are you crazy, Mr. Grant?"

"Not her. Your love of her! You cannot see it because you are under her spell. I see it."

Any man cannot resist the passion of that ghost.

"I'm telling you again, you're wrong, Mr. Grant.

"No, you can't see it! Your life has endured many trials, but it will burn like a feather, no matter how little you continue to excite that creature."

"I don't want her, Mr. Grant."

"But she does want you. She is a vampire, and she has nothing to give you! Do you understand?"

Rosales didn't answer anything. From the restroom, or beyond, came the young woman's voice:

"Will you leave me here by myself for a long time?"

In that instant, I suddenly remembered the skeleton lying there.

"The skeleton, Rosales!" I cried. "What has happened to the skeleton?"

"It came back," he answered. "It came back to nothing. But she is there now on the couch. Listen to me, Mr. Grant: no creature has ever imposed on her creator. I created a ghost; and, mistakenly, a rag of bones. You ignore some details of the creation. Hear them now. I bought a flashlight and projected our friend's tapes onto a screen that was very sensitive to N1 rays. Utilizing a simple device, I kept moving the photographic instants of the greatest life of the lady who awaits us. You know well that there are in all of us, as we speak, moments of such conviction, of inspiration so timely that we notice in the gaze of others. She detached herself from the screen, fluctuating a few millimeters at first, and finally came to me, just as you have seen her. This event occurred three days ago. She is there..."

The passive voice of the young woman reached us again from the bedroom:

"Will you come, Mr. Rosales?"

"Get rid of her, Rosales," I exclaimed, taking him by the arm, "before it's too late!"

"Good evening, Mr. Grant," he said with a smile,

bowing.

Well, this story is over. Did Rosales find strength in the world to resist? Very soon—maybe today—I'll find out.

The following day I wasn't surprised when a servant called me urgently on the phone, nor did I feel any surprise when I saw the curtains in the living room gilded by fire, and remains of burned films on the floor. Lying on the rug next to the couch, Rosales lay dead.

The servants knew that during the last night, Rosales transported the camera to the hall. The theory is that due to an oversight, the films burned, the sparks reaching the couch's cushions; therefore, the medics attributed the man's death to a heart injury precipitated by the heat.

I think something else happened. The calm expression on Rosales' face hadn't changed, and even his dead countenance retained its usual warm tone. But I am sure that there was not a drop of blood left in the depths of his veins.

THE PURITAN

The cinematographer's workshops, those studios around which millions of faces revolve in an orbit of never-satisfied curiosity and dreams never accomplished, have inherited from the abandoned painting workshop the legend of incredible feats on the altar of art.

On the one hand, the freedom of spirit familiar to great actors, and on the other, the very rich salaries that they earn, explain these festivals that not infrequently have the sole purpose of keeping the audience vibrant, before the fantastic, distant Hollywood stars.

Once the day's work is complete, everyone leaves the studio. Perhaps the technical employees continue their work throughout the night, and maybe one or ten kilometers away, the daily tumult continues in a party. But on the sets, in the studio proper, the silence now reigns.

This silence and the appearance of emptiness are traits of the central wardrobe, a vast hall whose façade, so broad that it would give way to three cars, opens onto the interior patio, onto the sizeable sand—grained square with all the workshops.

The cloakroom lies at the end of the square, and its large gate always remains open. Through the many leaves, on clear nights, the moon invades much of the dark hall. In that quiet room, where no soul can even hear the screeching of the loudest machines, we have our gathering late at night of the dead actors of the films.

The photographic impression on the tape, shaken by the speed of the machines, excited by the burning light of the spotlights, galvanized by the ongoing projection, has deprived our sad bones of the peace that should reign over them. We are dead, without a doubt, but our destruction is not total. An intangible survival, barely warm so as not to be made of ice, governs and animates our specters. Through the wardrobe, in peace, we wander in the light of the moon, without anxiety, without passions or memories. Something like a vague stupor hangs over our movements. We would seem like sleepwalkers, indifferent to each other, if the immediate gloom of the enclosure did not pretend a vague hall of a mansion, where the ghosts of what we have been continue a passable imitation of life.

We have not shaken the souls of the artists that survive us in vain; We have not let our hearts sleep in their arms a hundred times so that their present films are not the nocturnal commentary of our conciliators. Our own past—life, struggles, and love—is closed to us. Our existence starts with a camera shutter. We are an instant: perhaps imperishable, but a single spectral instant. The film and the projection deprived us of our eternal sleep, closed the world to us, off the screen, to any other interest.

Our gathering does not always bring together, however, all the visitors of the cloakroom. When someone misses the meeting, we already know that some theater is displaying one of his films.

"He's sick," we say. "He has stayed home."

The next night, or three or four later, the ghost returns to his usual place in the company he prefers. And although his countenance expresses fatigue and the fine ravages of a new projection are perceived in his silhouette, there are no traces of actual suffering in them.

It seems that during the time of the passage of the film, the actor fell into a state of semi-consciousness.

A very different thing happened with Ella (I don't want to provide her real name), the beautiful and vivid star, who one night made her entrance among us—dead.

The success that this actress achieved in life in her brilliant and fleeting meteor career is not news to anyone. Of any woman, she possessed the most

decadent qualities. The extreme beauty of the face, of her body, of her soul—
any one of these supreme gifts can by itself bring down a feminine soul with her excessive charm. She, almost as a punishment, possessed and endured all three.

She possessed everything in her brief passage through the world. She knew the follies of success, fortune, vanity, flattery, danger. Faith only denied her the foolishness of love.

Among all the men who surrendered to her, by her very side or through two thousand leagues of clamor and desire, she offered herself entirely to the only being capable of rejecting her: a puritan of inviolable moral principles, who before meeting the actress had placed his honor on his wife and their tender ten-month-old son.

It was not easy to guess the state of her feelings, but it would not have been pleasant for anyone to bear the shock that her simple principles freed in her heart with her guilty love.

She had met him in the studio, for the lucky mortal had a deep interest in movies. And although she had never reached out to stretch her lips to him, she knew well that, had she done so, he would have removed her arms from his neck, stiff and rigid as duty itself.

She knew well that he loved her, but not as a

man, but as a hero. And when a lover usurps for himself all the heroism of love, the other has nothing left but to die.

In short: the married man returned, bitter to the dregs, the cup of love that she held out to him with her body. And she, without the strength to resist, killed herself.

Suicidal, indeed, she could not enjoy peace, nor had her love and pain been forbidden to her. Her heart always beat, and in her eyes, deeply excavated, we could not guess what dose of arsenic or mortal love was still dilating them with anguish.

Because contrary to what happened with us, she lived a half-life. When a theater plays our films, we disappear from the gathering, as I have already mentioned. She does not. She was lying right there, wrapped in cold, her expression anxious and panting. We pretended not to notice her presence in such cases, but she sat up on the couch when the projection barely finished. She then expressed to us her distress.

"Oh, what anguish!" She told us, uncovering her forehead. "I'm sorry for everything I do as if I hadn't acted in the studio. Before, I knew that at the end of a scene, no matter how strong it might have been, I could think of something else and laugh. Not anymore! It's like I'm the character myself!"

Well. We had reached the end of our days, and we didn't owe anything to anybody. Ella cut her days short. Her unfinished life suffered a substantial deficit, her feigned pain.

She had to pay. Of her love, she had said nothing to us, until the night when at the end of her task she murmured bitterly:

"If only ... if only I could stop seeing him!"

Oh! We didn't need to remember either. For us to understand the suffering of the poor creature: night after night, after a month of complete disappearance from Hollywood, Mac Namara attended from the stalls of the theater, and without missing one, the films of Ella.

Never until today has literature taken full advantage of the extraordinary situation that occurred when a husband, a son, a mother, tun to see on the screen, throbbing with life, the loved one they lost. But neither was torture equal to that of a lover who finally sees herself surrender to the man for whom she killed herself. Who cannot run into his arms deliriously, cannot look at him, or even turn to him because all of her and their love are no longer more than a photographic spectrum.

Nor was it happiness what passed through the heart of the Puritan, whose wife and son slept peacefully but whose open eyes contemplated the actress alive.

For us, however, only Ella's situation was of lively interest. It is unfortunate to have died in vain when life still demands what it can no longer give.

"It is not possible," She sometimes murmured after seeing him leave, "to suffer more than I suffer!" Three-quarters of an hour watching him in the audience ...! And me here...!"

Insensibly, we had all forgotten our walks in the moonlight and our whispers without heat, to only contemplate that torment. We had a dark feeling that Ella could not resist the tortures she continued to inflict on herself with cruelty.

"Oh, die! And never to see him again!" She said to herself, pressing her face in her hands.

But Dougald Mac Namara did not take his eyes off Ella on the other side of the screen.

One night, at the sad hour, while Ella lay motionless on the couch, half-hidden by how many blankets we had been able to throw on her body, the young woman suddenly took her hands away from her eyes.

"He's not ..." she said slowly. "Today, he has not come."

The film's screening continued, but the actress no longer seemed to suffer from the passion of her characters. Everything had vanished into inert nothingness, leaving in compensation a path of livid and tremendous anguish, which went from an empty armchair to a ghostly couch.

Neither the next night, nor the next, nor those that followed for a month, Dougald Mac Namara returned.

Must I warn that from half an hour before the exhibition on all those nights, our lips remained mute and that from the first squeak of the film, our eyes did not leave Ella?

She was also waiting—and in what way!—From the very beginning of the projection. For a long time—the time of looking for him in the living room—her face, thinned by suicide, looked fantastic with eager hope. And when her eyes finally closed—Mac Namara hadn't come!

New nights followed, in vain. Nobody now occupied the usual seat of the theater.

In an austere home, a man of rigid principles must have watched over the dream of his chaste wife and his pure infant. When he has resisted a warm mouth that begs for a kiss, he opposes a dancing celluloid illusion very well. After a moment of weakness, Mac Namara would no longer return to the Monopole.

We believed so. Ella no longer expressed her wish to die; she was dying.

One night, finally, shortly after the projection began, and while we did not lose sight of her face, she separated her dead hands abruptly from her face.

Suddenly her face lit up with happiness to that radiant splendor that only life has the secret, and reaching out her arms; she cried out. But what a scream, oh God!

"She has seen him!" we said to ourselves. "He has returned to the Monopole!"

It was more. Over there, somewhere in the world, the rigidly principled Puritan had just shot himself.

So there is something superior to Death and Duty. Two steps from us, now, the lovers are close. The lovers won't ever be separated. He stifled his impure love, was temporarily defeated when he went to hide in the theater and returned at last in triumph to his austere home. He sits now next to her, on the couch.

She smiles in almost carnal bliss, pure as her death. She no longer owes nothing to destiny, and she rests in peace. She has fulfilled her wish.

VAMPIRISM

"Yes," said Attorney Rhode. "I know about it. It's a case, quite rare around here, of vampirism. Rogelio Castelar, an ordinary man, was found one night in the cemetery dragging the recently buried corpse of a woman. The individual shattered his hands because he had removed a cubic meter of soil with his nails. At the edge of the pit lay the remains of the coffin, freshly burned. And as a macabre complement, a cat, undoubtedly a stranger, was lying there with broken kidneys."

In the first interview with the man, I saw that I had to deal with a crazy macabre man. At first, he insisted on not answering me, although he did not stop for a moment to nod at my reasoning. Then, at last, he seemed to find in me a man worthy of hearing him. His mouth trembled with the anxiety to communicate.

"Ah! You understand me!" he exclaimed, fixing his feverish eyes on me. And he continued with great enthusiasm:

"I'll tell you everything! Yes! What was that

about the cat? Me! It was only me! Listen to me: When I arrived there, my wife ..."

"Where exactly?" I interrupted him.

"Right there ... So?... When I arrived, my wife ran like crazy to hug me. And immediately, she fainted. They all rushed over to me then, looking at me with crazy eyes. My home! It had burned, collapsed, sunk with everything in it! That, that was my house! But not her, my wife! Then a wretch devoured by madness shook my shoulder, yelling at me:"

"What are you doing? Answer me!"

And I replied:

"She's my wife! My wife is safe!"

Then a cry arose:

"It's not her! That's not your wife!"

"I felt that when I lowered my gaze to look at what I had in my arms, my eyes wanted to jump out of their sockets. Wasn't that Maria, my Maria, passed out? A stroke of blood lit my eyes, and a woman who was not Maria fell from my arms. So I jumped on a barrel and overpowered all the workers. And I shouted hoarsely:"

"Why! Why!"

"Not one of them had combed hair because the

wind blew their hair sideways. Many outside eyes were looking at me. Then I started hearing from everywhere:"

"She died"

"She died crushed."

"She screamed."

"She screamed just once."

"She died."

"His wife was crushed to death."

"By all the saints!" I screamed then, wringing my hands. "Let's save her, comrades! We must save her!"

"And we all ran. We all ran in silent fury to the rubble. The bricks flew, the frames fell out of place."

"At four, I was working by myself. I didn't have a healthy nail left, nor was there anything else to dig with my fingers. But the feeling on my chest! Anguish and fury of tremendous misfortune that trembled in my chest as I sought my Maria!"

"Only the piano remained to be removed. There was a deep silence around me, a fallen petticoat and dead rats. Under the lying piano, on the floor garnet of blood and coal, lay the crushed servant."

"I took her out to the patio, where there were

only four small walls, slimy with tar and water. The slippery floor reflected the dark sky. So I grabbed the maid and started dragging her around the yard."

"Those steps were mine. And what steps! One step, another step, another step!"

"In a doorway—filled with coal and nothing more—the house cat was huddled, which had escaped disaster, although it was in pain. The fourth time the maid and I passed by, the cat howled in anger."

"Ah! Wasn't it me, then?" I screamed desperately. Wasn't I the one who searched among the rubbles a single piece of my Maria!"

"The sixth time we passed the cat, the animal bristled. The seventh time it got up, dragging its back legs. And then it followed us, trying to dip its tongue into the servant's greased hair."

"That was the corpse of Maria, right, you bloody body snatcher!"

"Body snatcher!" I repeated, looking at him. "But then that happened in the cemetery, and what you're telling us isn't the truth!"

The vampire then flattened his hair while he looked at me with his eyes full of craziness.

"So you knew then!" He murmured. "So you all

know it, and you let me talk for an hour! Ah!" He roared in a sob, throwing his head back and sliding down the wall until he fell into a sitting position.

"I did not need to know more, as you understand," concluded the lawyer, "to make a decision. We immediately admitted him to the psychiatric institution. It's been two years since this, and last night they released him, perfectly cured."

"Last night?" exclaimed a young man in severe mourning. "And at night, the psychiatric institution discharges crazy people?"

"Why not? We cured the individual, and he is now as healthy as you and me. Besides, if he relapses, which is very common in these vampires, he must be doing the same things now. But this is not my concern. Good evening, gentlemen."

ABOUT THE AUTHOR

 Horacio Quiroga, born in 1878, was a prolific Uruguayan poet and short story writer. He wrote eight books containing over 100 short stories in total.

Horacio's personal life was very chaotic. His father's death at the age of two and the suicide of his step-father marked his childhood. However, when he came of age, he bought a small piece of land with his inheritance and married a beautiful young bride who inspired two of his most important works.

Horacio published his most famous short story-book, Jungle Tales, while living with his wife and two children in the jungle. After moving to Buenos Aires in 1917, Quiroga lived in a basement with his children as he worked on the stories that he later compiled into several books, the first being "Tales of Love, Madness, and Death," published in that same year.

Horacio Quiroga committed suicide on February

19, 1937.

ABOUT THE TRANSLATOR

Joaquin de la Sierra is the founder of Accomplisher.com, a digital education platform.

Besides working on his platform, Joaquin focuses much of his time translating Spanish books to English, fulfilling his mission of helping spread Latin American literature.

If you wish to support Joaquin's future projects, please sign up on this page, and he'll notify you when he launches a new project.

Printed in Great Britain
by Amazon

82024669R00098